DISCOVERING LIGHT

12 Steps Overcoming Anxiety and Depression without Medication

Aaron M. Anderson

DEDICATION

This book is dedicated to those who believed in me when I was completely down and out and showed nothing that warranted such belief—my parents, grandparents, friends, extended family, medical practitioners and therapists, my wife, and God. Without such an amazing supporting cast, I could never have finished the play. This book is also dedicated to the thousands of people struggling with anxiety and depression who don't know where to turn. You can overcome these struggles, and it is my hope and prayer that this book provides some light in your life showing you how to do so.

CONTENTS

CONTENTS

PREFACE

In my experience with friends, family, and others who suffer from anxiety and depression, I have discovered that each person has certain triggers that lead to severe anxiety oftentimes followed by depression. For me, it was relationships with women, which I later discovered stemmed from the abandonment I felt as a child, but for others, it can be a number of things—flying, driving, having children, speaking or performing in front of a group, keeping commitments, and so on.

Many people—including me, for many years—do not realize they have a problem; instead, they struggle and suffer much longer than they should. I applaud you for having the courage to recognize and accept that there is a problem and then take the next step, which is learning how to approach overcoming anxiety and depression.

It seems to me that in our society, doctors are quick to prescribe a pill and slow to try to find the root causes of an issue. We are conditioned to think that once we've identified a problem, we can pop a pill and it will be resolved.

I am not a medical professional, but my experience in overcoming anxiety and depression caused me to believe otherwise. My internal speech had become so negative that every time I hit a "trigger," I derailed into panic and depression. Over the course of a few years, I was finally able to overcome anxiety and depression completely by applying the 12 steps outlined in this book.

While I chose to attack anxiety and depression without medication, I am by no means saying that anyone is inferior for using medication; nor am I advocating that people should not use medication. Obviously, I would recommend speaking with a doctor before trying to go on or off of medication.

From personal experience and witnessing others dealing with anxiety and depression, I have seen that doctors and counselors usually recommend some form of cognitive or other type of therapy whether or not the patient chooses to go on medication. Those

I spoke with who took medication told me that they felt their minds were "clouded" and they lost the desire to take the time to reprogram and relearn thought patterns to replace those that lead to anxiety and depression. Therefore, I am a strong advocate of non-medicinal approaches to overcoming anxiety and depression.

I want to emphasize that whether or not you choose to take medication, it will require an enormous amount of patience, desire, vision, and effort on your part and also that of loved ones in your life. It can definitely be accomplished though. I'm living proof of that.

I know that if you set your mind to overcoming anxiety and depression and use the steps outlined in part 2 of this book, you will see significant changes in your life. I was able to get my life back again and am now living a normal and productive life. Dreams, such as marriage, children, and a good job, became a reality in my life. I feel that I am truly blessed.

The first portion of the book, entitled "Discovering Light," is a semi-fictional narrative of some of the struggles I faced and the ways I approached overcoming anxiety and depression. The reason why I say semi-fictional is because some of the experiences I share in the narrative aren't exactly as they occurred and names have been changed as well. The feelings and situations though are completely accurate.

The first section of the book is designed to show people who suffer from anxiety and depression that they are not alone, the thoughts that go through their heads are real, and that this is something others struggle with as well. For those who do not suffer but who may have a loved one who does, my hope is that this portion of the book provides a glimpse into what goes on inside the head of someone who is struggling with anxiety and depression.

Part 2 of the book "Twelve Steps to Overcoming Anxiety and Depression without Medication" is designed specifically for those who struggle. The experiences I share in this section are completely accurate and contain more information on the various methods used in overcoming anxiety and depression than Part 1. There are helpful resources and insights that proved invaluable for me in my journey to being anxiety and depression free. Keep in mind there is a lot of information in this section, and those who struggle with severe anxiety should avoid the tendency to try to tackle all the suggestions at once. I recommend just trying a couple of the suggestions at first and adding others a little at a time. It would be quite easy to feel overwhelmed if you look at everything all at once and try to tackle it all head-on without pacing yourself.

It is my hope that some, if not all, of these steps will provide some insight and guidance for those who are struggling with overcoming anxiety and depression, whether or not they choose to use medication.

God bless you in your journey to overcome anxiety and depression. You can do this!

ACKNOWLEDGMENTS

I am grateful to several key people who have helped me and encouraged me in writing this book: Becca, my beautiful bride, who has provided support and encouragement; Daren Falter, whose insight into writing has helped immensely; my parents and other family members (in particular one of my uncles, one of my aunts, and one of my brothers who struggle with anxiety and depression themselves); friends who helped me along the way; and finally, my two beautiful children "Babes" and "Buddy," who are the fruits of my being able to overcome anxiety and depression and are an inspiration and motivation to me daily.

Part One:
Discovering Light

1
PEAKS AND VALLEYS

He couldn't do it anymore. He ran outside into the pelting rain and got into his car. After locking the door, he pounded his fist into the steering wheel. Tears came down like the rain hitting his windshield as he sobbed.

Thoughts swirled around in his head of how he had been the one everyone always looked to for advice and friendship. Although a young man, only in his late twenties, he had successfully traveled the world, earned a master's degree, found corporate success, and been well-liked by women. Yet, there he was, alone in his car. He beat himself up in his head even more as he watched the teardrops hit the steering wheel and drip to the floor.

Just days earlier, he had found out something, something that he didn't want anyone else to know. However, over the past few years, he had been finding it more and more difficult to keep it a secret. The image he was trying to portray was cracking like a weathered statue, and what he had been hiding underneath would be exposed. How could he face his friends and family? The world in general? Where could he look for help? Furthermore, what would they say and think about him once he told them?

Maybe it would just be easier to end the whole thing. Life, in general, was too hard. The burden he carried was much too heavy. The idea of leaving the world seemed so freeing, and for a moment, he fell into self-indulgent thoughts of ending it in some way. He pictured his soul leaving his tortured body and floating freely up into the air, looking down at all the worries and struggles this world had brought him. Sure, he would miss his friends and family, but they wouldn't miss him, really—would they? Especially when they found out that all these years what they had thought was him had been a façade, that he was a fake. Phony. They would probably be glad to see him go, he thought.

Suddenly, his thoughts turned to those who depended on him, and reality set in. He also began to think of his belief that the same spirit and way we think in this life carries on to the next. The thought of carrying this heavy burden into another life was too much. He lifted his head up and tried to look through the window as the rain came down even harder against the windshield. He couldn't see anything besides small rivers of rain trickling down. As he sat alone with his thoughts, he noticed a small break in the clouds and one ray of light dance down onto the pavement and up onto the hood of his car.

With no alternatives, feeling desperate but with a small glimmer of hope inside, he decided to take a step into the unknown.

2
GUIDANCE

"Dear God," he quietly whispered, "I'm hurting right now. Thoughts of ending my life torment me inside my head, and I want to end it. I'm physically and emotionally tired and can't go on. I have read that Your Son was lifted up on the cross to take our burdens for us, and I need You to do that now. I have a small bit of faith that You can do this, but I will need a miracle. My preference is that You remove this weight right away. I can't do it anymore. I am under too much pressure and feel as though I am carrying the world on my shoulders. I feel I have no choice but to move forward, but I cannot do it alone anymore. Please help me."

He sat with his eyes closed for a moment. Even though he didn't see anyone around, it felt good to talk out loud and share his feelings. He hoped that there was a God who had listened to his prayer, but for the moment, he was just content to feel a little better.

Moments before, he had done something he had never done in his life. The stress and pressure from working a sales job in corporate America had become too much, especially since he had started having these crazy "episodes." He didn't know what to call them, but sporadically and spontaneously, he would suddenly start breathing heavily, his chest would start to hurt, thoughts would swirl in his head, and he would desperately try to catch his breath. Crazy thoughts would spin around and around in his head, and just as he thought he was going to lose his mind or pass out, it would stop.

What didn't stop though were his thoughts afterward. He would worry about when the next episode was going to hit him. He would also worry that his coworkers might have seen him having these episodes. Sometimes as he worried, he could feel it start coming back again, and sometimes it did. Like a surfer falling off a wave and rolling end over end, not knowing which way was up, he would fall back into the swirling thoughts, and then it would stop again. This time he would feel a heaviness, a sinking weight of despair that would cause him to stare off into open space. He would then feel physically unable to move.

That day, he had decided he couldn't take it anymore and did what he had never done before. He had simply sent an e-mail to his boss and coworkers thanking them for their acquaintance over the years, packed his office supplies, and walked out of the building—quitting his job. At first, he had felt such freedom, but as he went outside, guilt and reality had set in and he beat himself up inside for being so ir-responsible. It was in that moment that he had stepped into the un-known and prayed.

His thoughts were suddenly interrupted by a noise coming from the alley behind him. This was not the best part of town, and he usu-ally got in his car quickly and left. That day, however, he had stayed. He was looking out his driver's side window to see what it was when *bam*! Something hit his passenger side window.

3
THE MESSENGER

Instantly, his thoughts turned to someone trying to break in and mug him. His heart jumped to his throat as he whirled to the right to look out the passenger-side window. He was relieved to see someone he hadn't seen in years. It was David, his old friend and former roommate.

"Hey, Michael! Are you going to let me in or keep me out here in the cold rain?" David said.

Michael came to his senses and opened the door.

"You look like a mess, man!" David observed. "How about we get out of the rain and into somewhere warm…a coffee shop or something. We need to catch up!"

* * *

Michael sat in the chair watching David at the counter. David had always been a good friend. He remembered the parties they went to, the girls they had dated, and the late nights they had stayed up analyzing potential relationships with those girls and the subsequent breakups. He remembered the road trips, parties, and all their friends. David had always been a fun guy, and people liked him.

One of the things that had brought them so close together was their similar histories. On the first day they met, they had instantly hit it off and talked for hours. One thing led to another, and soon they were talking about their upbringing. Both were the eldest children and had similar situations with their families. As the oldest children, they had felt, growing up, that they were the protectors of their siblings—especially when one or both of their parents were being abusive.

Michael had related how his mother had disowned him after his parents' divorce when he was eleven. She had told him she didn't want to talk with him again. He had felt abandoned and angry, as though someone had ripped a piece of him out. David had empathized and relayed a story of his father abandoning the family. After that initial discussion, they had agreed not to discuss it anymore and especially not with other people.

Although that topic remained off-limits, it had always been clear to Michael that David harbored pain and frequently experienced a deep sense of sadness and despair, especially in the quiet moments when no one was around.

That day, however, there was something special about him. He seemed to have an extra skip in his step. Michael had never seen him this happy before. Maybe it was just because it had been two years since they had seen each other.

"So," said David as he sat down with a hot drink for each of them, "what have you been up to the last couple years?"

Michael spent a few minutes catching him up on the major highlights of his life, which included mostly girls, work, church, and school. He had finished his master's degree in business administration just a few months earlier and was very relieved to have accomplished that. He volunteered at his church as the young men's group leader, spending about twenty hours per week there. He had grown to love and respect the young men, and he cared for them collectively and individually. He had been very successful at work over the past few years, rising from the bottom of the rung on the sales team to become a national sales trainer for the company. They would fly him around the country to conduct training for new sales associates.

When he started talking about Mei, he broke down a bit. Mei was the most beautiful girl he had ever been with. Images of her lovely features and her engaging eyes and the memory of the warmth of her touch and the bond they had felt flooded through him.

"Are you okay, brother?" asked David. "I remember you guys had something good going on. Tell me what happened."

Michael went on to describe the situation and nearly choked up a few times. He recalled all the things they liked doing together: tennis, hiking, biking, watching the sun set, embracing, kissing…everything. Above and beyond all of the things they did together was the way they could just talk for hours about anything. They could laugh, cry, and be serious. It seemed perfect.

Michael's expression turned from wistful to sad as his thoughts abruptly shifted to how they had ended the relationship.

"Whoa, man! You can't stop there! Don't tell me you broke up with another girl!" said David incredulously.

Michael had a long history of short relationships with women. In fact, he was lucky to last more than a few dates. Throughout the years, David and his other buddies had teased him for being such a ladies' man. At first, Michael had started using girls as a game of sorts. It was something of a contest to see how many he could get to like him. Over time, it became a habit, and even when he really liked the girl he was with, he couldn't quite commit to a relationship and would use her and then break up with her. Outwardly, he gave the appearance of bravado and confidence, but inwardly, he was very insecure and felt that if he got too close to a girl, she would leave him. After all, the closest female person in his life had chosen to leave him. Why should he let someone else in?

"Yeah," Michael said, "I broke up with her."

"What was wrong with this one?" asked David.

"Nothing," said Michael. "That's the problem. There is nothing wrong with her. She is perfect in every way."

"So why did you do it?" his friend asked.

"How much time do you have, old friend?" Michael answered.

"I have as much time as you need, bro!"

"Well, in that case, let me think a second about where to start."

Michael leaned back in his chair and put his hands behind his head as images came flooding into his mind.

4
DISCOVERY

There she was, across the way, one of the most beautiful women he had ever laid eyes on. There were many people between them, but he was determined to meet her. He looked directly at her across the room and through the crowd, somehow, their eyes connected. She had a sparkle in her eye that seemed so inviting. He couldn't think of anything besides meeting her. Slowly, but with confidence, he worked his way through the crowd. She was still there and cast a shy glance his way to let him know he was welcome. He walked up to her, and she turned and looked up at him.

"Michael!" David said.

"Oh! Yeah, sorry, man. I was just thinking of the first time we met. Let me get back to telling you what happened…So you remember the first day she and I met, right?" Michael said. "You know, at that big party?"

"Boy, do I ever!" said David. "Man, you were smooth at that party, weren't you? Going up to her and introducing yourself to her only to find that you had already met her a couple weeks before."

They both chuckled.

"Yeah, that wasn't the smoothest introduction I've ever had," said Michael.

"I remember though that you recovered well, and after a couple weeks, it seemed to be working so well."

He was right. After the introduction and a few more conversations, Michael and Mei spent a lot of time together. Outwardly, they were a perfect couple. Inwardly, Michael had very uneasy feelings about getting too committed. Every couple of months, he would start analyzing their relationship, and doubts would arise—what if they became too close and she left him? This led him to more drastic worries, and he would start panicking inside. After the panic was over, he would feel very dark and discouraged and emotionally separate himself from Mei.

After a few months of this, Mei decided that it would be best for both of them if they took a break, so she volunteered to help under-privileged orphans in a third-world country for a year.

"I remember that you guys seemed to be kind of up and down, but overall pretty good," said David. "I was surprised when you de-cided to take a break. She's back by now though, isn't she?"

"She is," said Michael.

"So are you guys together or what?" David asked.

"Well, we were, but now we're not," Michael answered. "It's hard to explain."

"Well, let's go back to the part where she left and catch me up on that," suggested David.

"Okay," said Michael, as he once again started reminiscing.

It was a perfect summer evening. They held each other as the ocean waves lapped gently against the shore. The sun was glimmer-ing across the waves and followed them up past the trees where they were sitting. No one was around except for the seals and the seabirds in the distance. It was a moment that Michael wanted to freeze in time. He gently reached down and stroked Mei's cheek. She looked up at him, and her eyes sparkled like the ocean waters next to them. They kissed gently. Michael felt the electric warmth and love flow through him like he had many times before with her.

"How do you feel?" he asked her.

"Melted…" she quietly responded as she squeezed him tighter.

Michael's thoughts fast-forwarded to the day after Mei had left. He started talking to David again.

"The day after she left, I went down to the beach and sat where we had spent many evenings together. I watched the birds, listened to the waves, watched the sun dance across the water, and it all swelled up inside of me how much I loved and missed her.

"I cried," he confessed. "I cried hard. In fact, I wrote down the lyrics to a song as I was crying."

As he said this, his mind flashed back to the first time he had ever played a song he had written for a girl in public. It was down-town along the Seattle waterfront in a coffee shop. The misty sea air surrounded a group of people who had gathered around to hear him and some other people play an acoustic set. When he got up, he noticed quite a few pretty girls in the audience, but the one who stood out above the crowd was sitting in the front row. Her beautiful blue eyes beamed up at him, just as they had the first day they had met.

Michael adjusted the microphone, leaned into it, looked right into Mei's eyes, and said, "This song was written about someone in the audience." He winked at her and started playing and singing.

"Subtly and softly, you've crept into my heart. Without a warning, I woke with a start. And in that moment, that perfect moment, the sun shone in your eyes. I surrendered as we embraced. There was no more disguise…How can you turn the sky from blue? I'd do it all again to be with you…"

As Michael looked up after singing the first verse and chorus, he noticed a lot of the girls in the audience seemed to like the song, but he only cared about the one who was beaming and grinning from ear to ear in the front row.

He felt so good remembering that moment. Suddenly, his thoughts were interrupted.

"You always were the romantic, weren't you?" said David. "Remember that time you wrote her a song and sang it to her in that coffee shop?"

"Oh yes, I'll never forget that!" Michael responded. "Could you tell I was just thinking about that night? That was the first time I ever played my guitar in public. She was very surprised, but flattered, to say the least."

"Dude!" interjected David. "How can you let someone like that go?"

"Those were my thoughts exactly as I sat on the beach the day after she left," he said. "I decided in that moment that I wasn't going to let a day go by without showing her I loved her. I committed to writing her letters each week since she would rarely be in a place to take phone calls."

"So did you keep that promise you made to yourself?"

"I did." Michael nodded. "I wrote to her every week for a year. Not only did I write to her, but I also recorded songs for her and sent them too."

"So what happened when she got back?" asked David.

"Well," said Michael, "that is where all of this started."

5
INTRUSION

He couldn't believe it. After all this time, he was still having these feelings. His head was spinning around and around. He tried to breathe slowly and steadily but ended up gasping. He looked up, but everything seemed blurry. He got up and stumbled around until he found the bathroom. Looking into the mirror, he despised what he saw—a weak, helpless man who could not control anything in his life. He saw a confused soul who couldn't even breathe normally.

He turned on the water and splashed his face. Ahhh…the cool water felt so good on his burning forehead. The thoughts and feelings started to subside, and then the numb, empty feeling began to settle in. This seemed to be happening more frequently without any explanation whatsoever. He felt heavy and empty inside. He didn't want to go back out, but he had to. After a few minutes, he decided to go out and face his demons.

"Are you okay?" asked Mei.

"Yeah, I'm fine," Michael said. "I just had a dizzy spell, is all."

"Well," she said, "what do you want to do?"

Michael felt completely drained emotionally, physically, and mentally. He really just wanted to curl up on his bed and sleep—just let this all pass away.

"How about we go to my place," he suggested instead.

"Well, that's fine," she said. "Anything is good as long as we're together."

Michael wished he could say the same thing. He felt so guilty inside and ashamed. Where did these feelings come from? Why couldn't he just be normal?

It had been just over a year since they had seen each other. Throughout the whole time she was gone, he had felt fine. In fact, he had felt even more connected to her and had grown to know a whole new side of her through her letters. They had shared deep feelings, personal goals, and how life in general was going. He had chosen not to date any other girls and had waited for her to return. Now she was back, and somehow, he couldn't be normal around her.

As they walked back into his apartment, Michael wondered why these feelings rushed through him every time he was with Mei. He looked over at her. She was even more beautiful than he remembered. Her glossy brown hair, her blue eyes that sparkled with joy upon seeing him, and her engaging personality were all characteristics he had always wanted in a girl. In fact, she was the only girl he had ever truly loved.

Love. What does that mean exactly, and where does that lead to? he thought. *It leads to commitment, marriage, and ultimately her leaving. I have to let her go before she hurts me.* His thoughts began to spin out of control, and his heart started pounding in his chest again. He had to lean against the counter and catch his breath again.

"We're going to have to break things off," Michael said abruptly.

Mei looked up at him completely stunned. She seemed to have shattered inside. What about all of the things he had said in his letters? What about the dreams they had shared? What about the children he had told her they would have together?

She knew he had been going through some emotional problems, but she desperately wanted to help.

"We can work things out, right?" she said, reaching out to him and pulling him closer.

It felt so good to have her close by his side. For just a moment in time, Michael felt free again. He held her closer and engaged in the embrace. They held each other in silence, not sure exactly what to say or do. After a few minutes of silence, Mei looked up at Michael, and when their eyes connected, they could no longer resist; they leaned in and passionately kissed each other, letting their worries fade away.

* * *

"So you had some crazy feelings, but you ended up okay in the end, right?" David said as Michael concluded the description of the evening Mei returned.

"Well, for the moment, it was fine," he said, hesitating, "but I just couldn't shake the feelings I would have every time we were together."

"What do you mean?"

"I felt trapped," Michael started. "I felt caught between what I truly wanted intellectually and emotionally and the severe panic I felt inside when I thought about committing to a serious relationship."

"That doesn't make any sense, bro," his friend said.

"If it had made sense, things would be different," Michael responded sadly. "Every time I was with her, I would feel a rush of confusion and thoughts coming into my head about the future. My heart would race, my head would spin, and I would feel as if I were having a heart attack or something. Then I would sink deep into a negative emotional state. I would feel completely drained, and all I wanted to do was stare at the wall or lay in my bed for hours. I finally just couldn't deal with it anymore."

"Man, that's crazy!" David said. "So what did you do?"

"I ended it."

"You what?" shouted David. People in the coffee shop turned around to see what the loud noise was.

David took notice and lowered his voice to a loud whisper. "You *what*? How?"

"It was kind of lame," said Michael as he looked down at his cup, "but I did it over the phone."

"Dude! That's the lamest thing I've ever heard of!" he agreed, his voice rising again.

"It was the hardest thing I've ever done, but it was necessary to do it that way, because every time I was with her, I couldn't resist her." Michael's thoughts drifted.

He was sitting all alone on his bed sobbing uncontrollably. He looked over at his dresser where a picture of him and Mei stood. He threw it on the ground, shattering the glass. He looked at her letters and threw them out, yelling as he did. He felt torn inside, as if a piece of him had been ripped out. Unsure of what to do, he ran outside into the pouring rain. Not knowing where to go or caring where he ended up, he ran and ran until his lungs burned and his skin stung from the cold rain pelting him. When he couldn't run anymore, he collapsed onto the ground unaware and unconcerned that he was drenched.

He shut his eyes as the dark feelings he had been experiencing so frequently lately consumed him.

He was numb on the outside, but inside, he was dead. He stared blankly at the rain trickling down a leaf and dropping onto the ground right in front of his face. He then jealously watched the ground swallow up the drop of water. How he longed to be swallowed up and just forget about everything! The last remaining light of day turned to dusk. Dusk turned to dark as he closed his eyes and gave in to the sweet release of slumber.

6
RELAPSE

"Bzzzzz…bzzzz…bzzzz!" screeched the alarm. Michael abruptly woke up and slapped the clock. It crashed to the floor.

He was late for work again, but he didn't care. Nothing seemed to matter lately. Everything seemed to take so much energy—even simple things like eating, breathing, walking from one room to the other, let alone working and hanging out with friends.

Friends? Ha! What friends? If they really knew the true me, they wouldn't like me. In spite of such thoughts, Michael somehow mustered the energy to pick himself up out of bed and get ready for work. A few minutes later, he was on his way.

As he drove toward the city center, he passed the ocean. It used to be a view he looked forward to seeing, but now, it only reminded him of failure. Feelings of frustration, guilt, and rage rose inside him like a giant wave only to come crashing down to feelings of numbness, indifference, and apathy.

It had been months since he and Mei had broken up, and they hadn't spoken in all that time either. He had seen her as the most precious gift from God, and he had disrespected her. No, worse—he had abused her…just like he had done so many times before.

Why do I do this to girls? he asked himself. *What makes me bring them in and then freak out and push them away? Or is it something wrong with them?*

He was still deep in thought as he walked into his office building and sat down at his desk.

It had become a daily ritual. He would sit and stare at the computer screen for a long time, just trying not to think. Thoughts were dangerous. All too often lately, one thought would lead to another thought, and it would all start spinning into a crescendo of chaos and fury only to crash down into the depths of darkness and numbness, almost as if it were depression.

Depression! he thought and lifted his head up off the desk. *What if it's depression?*

There was no way it could be depression. That was for weak people who clearly couldn't control themselves or anything else around them. He had heard of people in his family suffering from depression, but he secretly and pridefully thought they were just trying to make excuses for their life situations—using depression as a scapegoat and an excuse to escape from reality.

But what if it is depression? I doubt it, but what if it is? Great! All I need now is a diagnosis of depression and I'll really be a freak!

Part of him wanted to find out, and another part of him didn't. For a few minutes, he wavered back and forth between looking up information about depression online and just forgetting about it.

Curiosity won. He found a website on depression that had an assessment people could do to discover if they had it and if so how "depressed" they were.

Twenty minutes later, he clicked the "assessment complete" button and waited for results. He turned and looked out his office window, which overlooked the water and the city below. He remembered a time when he had thought that was beautiful, but lately, he just felt like sleeping and barely had the energy to do anything. He turned back to see the score, and his heart sank to the bottom of his chest.

The ninety-fifth percentile! This can't be right! he thought.

He read further down the assessment results and sank back into his chair, completely discouraged. Not only did it show that he had severe depression, but he also had anxiety levels that were off the charts.

Suddenly, his thoughts turned to what depression *and* anxiety could mean for him. His mind started racing from one thought to the next as he pictured his life spinning out of control and ultimately leading him into a dark cellar in some insane asylum where he would rock back and forth numb from the tranquilizing medication. His heart raced and head spun as he frantically looked around the office to see if anyone had noticed. Afraid that people might see him for the weak person he was, he bolted from his office, ignoring friendly gestures from his coworkers, and ran out to his car. He had to get to the only place he knew to seek help.

7
THE FIX

"Thank you for seeing me, Doctor," said Michael as Dr. Rogers shut the door quietly behind him.

"Anytime, Michael," he answered and sat down at his desk. "What brings you in today?"

Michael went on to describe everything that had happened over the course of the last few years—the severe anxiety leading into thoughts spinning out of control and then into a full-blown panic attack followed by depression. The doctor sat back and listened quietly. After a few minutes, Michael finished and looked up at him.

Taking a few moments to formulate a reply, Dr. Rogers looked down at his notes, twirled his pen in his hands, and then said, "I can write you a prescription for an anxiety and depression drug, if you want." He took out his pen to write out the prescription.

Michael had expected more guidance and perhaps some counseling. Sure, a "quick fix" was tempting, but he wanted to know more about the drug and how it worked.

"So that's it? Pop a pill and I'm good to go?" he said dubiously.

"Oh, there are some side effects you should be made aware of, but the drug helps bring you into a state in which you can focus," Dr. Rogers answered.

"What are the side effects?" Michael asked.

"Well, although these effects don't happen with everyone, some of them are: increased anxiety, decreased appetite, nausea, insomnia, decreased sexual drive, agitation, and restlessness," Dr. Rogers informed him. "In addition, the first few weeks, you'll probably have to fight through some weird feelings as your chemistry adjusts to the medication."

"So if I run the risk of getting more panic attacks, what's the point in taking it? Weird chemistry?" Michael wondered out loud.

The doctor then backtracked and started explaining how the effects were rare and he would start out with a low dose so there was no need to worry.

However, Michael's mind was already racing.

More anxiety? How would that pan out? What if his thoughts spun even more and more out of control and life in general got out of hand?

He could see himself already with even more anxiety and frequent panic attacks, and his life seemed to be heading toward chaos. Suddenly, he felt it happening; he was starting to sweat. His thoughts became disordered and raced frantically as he felt his body giving way to a panic attack. He sat down and asked for some water before the full force of it hit. Although he wasn't completely sold on taking the pills, he didn't know where else to turn and he was desperate.

"So where do I go for the pills?" he asked.

Dr. Rogers filled out his prescription, and a few hours later, he was standing at his kitchen counter eyeballing the small pill. He looked at it closely and talked directly to it.

"So you're going to cure me, eh? How are you going to do that? What side effects are you going to give me? Well, here we go!"

And he popped the pill right into his mouth and swallowed.

Instantly, he felt strange. The sensation started in his throat and moved down throughout his body. It was one he was not accustomed to and found hard to describe. He didn't feel completely sick, but he did feel a sharp numbness.

This must be what the doctor meant when he said there would be an adjustment period, Michael thought.

Although it was a strange feeling, he decided to try it a few more times.

* * *

Time passed, and he was still feeling the same way each time he took the pill. The sensation would work its way throughout his body, leaving him numb and uneasy. Furthermore, his thoughts were racing even more as he wondered if this pill would give him more side effects. He decided to go to a psychologist specializing in depression to get a second opinion.

The first session with the psychologist went well. She was understanding and very helpful, providing tips on how to deal with depression and anxiety. However, one thing in particular stuck out in his mind. The psychologist had said that regardless of whether Michael took medication or not, he would need some cognitive therapy in order to get over the problem. Essentially, he would have to reprogram his way of thinking. He had also learned that there was a downside to medication: your body could get very accustomed to it, causing its effects to eventually wear off.

He concluded after the visit with the psychologist that if he had to work on his cognitive behavior anyway, there was no point in taking the drugs.

The next morning before he left for work, he threw away all his pills. As he watched them drop into the trash, he wondered if he was throwing away his last opportunity to overcome depression and anxiety.

* * *

There he was staring blankly at his computer screen again. He had just had another episode and didn't know if he could do it anymore. He had received an e-mail from his boss demanding better results and reminding him of the numbers he was supposed to be hitting. He used to care, but now he didn't. All he wanted to do was get well again, and this job was causing too much stress in his life.

Stress. That was the underlying cause for anxiety, he had read. A crazy thought then entered his mind: *How would life be without this job?*

He pictured a weight being lifted from him as he imagined life without the job. The more he thought about it, the better he felt. He typed up an e-mail to send back to his boss with a letter of resignation. He almost sent it but decided to check one more thing.

He pulled up his bank account online; he wanted to gauge how far the money he had saved could take him. As he averaged the numbers against his monthly spending, he felt a sense of elation and freedom he hadn't felt for a long time.

"Nine months!" he almost shouted out loud. "I can live for nine months on my savings!"

He pushed send, packed his stuff, and walked out the door. Moments later, it hit him.

What if I get sick and don't have insurance? What about those who rely on me? What will girls say about a guy with no job?

The thoughts kept swirling around in his mind. His heart raced, and his breathing increased as he rushed outside into the pouring rain and into his car.

* * *

"And that is where you hit my window and nearly scared me to death," Michael finished explaining the situation to David.

"Well, you've been through a lot," said David. "I'm proud of you for making this discovery though. You've taken the first step toward recovery. I'll give you the next one."

David reached into his bag and pulled something out.

8
THE GIFT

"Here it is!" he said as he plopped it down on the counter.

Michael was intrigued. It was a blue-and-white folder with some fluffy writing on it that said something about overcoming anxiety and depression.

"This program changed my life," David said.

Michael remembered how David had been a fun person, but he would sometimes struggle with similar problems dealing with stress and would also have bouts of depression.

"These are CDs with experts in the field and normal people like you and me, discussing how they were able to overcome anxiety and depression without drugs. There's also a workbook. I was able to get over my problems with anxiety and depression within a few months by applying the concepts in the program."

Michael was still thinking about the possibility of being healed from anxiety and depression without having to use medication. He pictured his life getting back to normal without the panic attacks, thoughts spinning out of control, weariness followed by depression and, at times, thoughts of suicide. He remembered how awful he had felt trying to take medication, but not knowing what else to do.

Was it true? Could someone truly get over anxiety and depression without drugs?

David could see the wheels turning inside his friend's head and thought it would be a good time to educate him on the program.

"The key to success with this program is that you need to really stick with it. There are twelve CDs here and lessons in the book that correspond with each CD. Each CD is to be used two to three times per week. Start with CD one and listen to it two to three times during the first week. Then move on to CD two in week two and so on."

"That's it?" said Michael.

"No, there's more." David pulled out another CD. "This CD is probably one of your most important CDs. You will need to use this one at least three times per day in the beginning. It is the most important CD in helping you train yourself to relax and to keep your thoughts from spinning out of control. Your thoughts control your actions, and if your thoughts are always full of stress and anxiety, they will manifest themselves in the form of panic and anxiety."

Michael had heard that idea before, but could it really be as simple as that? It sounded like when the doctor had told him that popping the pills would make it all okay. However, he was willing to give it a try. There weren't any other options on the table, and David looked better than he ever had before.

"Do you want to borrow it, brother?" David asked.

"Yes!" Michael exclaimed a bit more enthusiastically than he would have liked.

"Then here you go." David slid it across the table and stood up. "I've gotta run, but you can keep it as long as you need."

"Thank you," said Michael. "Thank you so much."

As he drove home, his optimism quickly fled, and thoughts from the day began spinning around his head again. *Why did you quit? What were you thinking? You're such an idiot! How do you think you can overcome anxiety and depression without drugs? You're such a loser!*

When he arrived at home, he quickly tossed everything aside and flopped down on the bed.

Michael had lain awake for a few hours in bed, trying to get to sleep, but finally decided it was useless. Even when he did drift off into sleep, the thoughts still haunted him in his dreams. He would wake up every hour or so tossing and turning. It had been months… years, perhaps, since he had received sufficient rest.

He rolled over and looked at the CDs on his desk. Could those really help him relax? It sounded too simple. Was it just his thoughts that were causing this, or was it a chemical imbalance, as the doctor had suggested?

After a few minutes of deliberation, he made the decision to give the CDs a try. He reached for the relaxation CD and turned it on.

Soft music and voices filled the room. He followed the person's instructions as they guided him to relax his muscles, focus his thoughts on the music, and turn off his inside voice. The music was so soothing;

he felt something he hadn't felt in a long time. Tension in his muscles seemed to seep into the springs of his bed and leave the room. Soon, he was sitting on a beach surrounded by nothing but the soothing waves and sun warming his whole body. He felt peaceful, confident, and, most important, relaxed.

He also sensed someone playing with his hair and caught a familiar scent that made him feel completely at peace. The hands moved gently from his hair and traced his face before finally crossing into a warm embrace across his chest. The skin felt familiar to his touch, and he lay back closer to the person. She then whispered softly into his ear, and he knew who it was…it was Mei.

"Ring! Ring!" Michael jumped out of bed as his phone rang.

He looked at his clock and saw it was already 10:00 a.m. He had to do a double-take—10:00 a.m.! Nine hours had passed. He hadn't slept that long in years. Better yet, he was refreshed and felt like a new man.

Maybe these CDs are effective, Michael thought as he popped one of the anxiety CDs into his player. He was fully on board with going through the program now.

An hour later, he felt very motivated. He had just listened to the first CD of the program and was surprised at how good he felt. Although the people talking weren't there in person, he felt as if they completely understood him. The program included people who had struggled with anxiety and depression talking with each other about their situations and how they were able to overcome them. The amazing thing was that the struggles came to people in all walks of life. One person had suffered for forty years before he found out how to treat anxiety without drugs.

For the first time in years, Michael felt a sense of hope and firmly believed he could overcome anxiety and depression without drugs.

9
THE KEY

"Ring! Ring!" the alarm went off again. Michael rolled over and noticed the time. *I'm late for work!* he thought and jumped out of bed, hurrying to get ready.

Halfway through his shower, it suddenly hit him. "What am I doing?"

He had forgotten that he had quit his job. Then the thoughts started to come. *What were you thinking? How are you going to survive without a job? Who will hire you knowing you walked out of your last job? What if you can't get another job? You will be out on the street then. How will life on the street be for you?* His mind was reeling, and his heart was pounding. He didn't want to be out on the street.

He pictured himself cold and shivering, standing on the side of the road during the day holding up a sign asking for food or money and then living under a bridge at night fighting off other homeless people for the best spot. He pictured stepping on a drug needle and getting AIDS.

His head began spinning, and suddenly, he felt very dizzy. Frantically, he turned off the shower and jumped out. He had to do something. He felt like he was having a heart attack. Should he call a doctor? A friend? He felt like he was about ready to die.

What if no one notices I'm dead? The thought hit him as he stumbled out of the bathroom.

Suddenly, he saw something and it snapped him out of his torture. It was a package he had received but left lying unopened on the floor by the TV. It was addressed to him, so he opened it.

The workout videos!

He had totally forgotten he had ordered workout videos. He had read about how important exercise was for people with depression and anxiety, but his heart was already pounding so hard and his head was so clouded with scary thoughts that he didn't feel like exercising.

He thumbed through the videos and noticed one about yoga. He had never done yoga before. He had heard that it was hard, yet relaxing.

I could use some relaxing, he thought and turned on the video.

Calm music filled the air as the instructor quietly shared thoughts and instructions on various yoga poses. Soon, Michael noticed his mind and heart starting to slow down. No longer did he feel frantic and out of control. He felt confident and in control.

An hour later, Michael was lying on the floor with his eyes closed, completely relaxed in both mind and spirit. Every time he had a panic attack, it exhausted him, and he would spin into negative thoughts and depression. This time, he was exhausted but also completely relaxed. The crazy thoughts had been replaced with soothing thoughts.

Waves lapped gently along the shoreline of the beach, and he heard the seabirds in the distance. A gentle hand stroked his hair, and he looked up to see loving eyes looking down at him. He couldn't quite tell who she was, but the smell and her features were so familiar. He knew it must be Mei. Warmth and love filled his soul, and he moved in closer as she held him more tightly. He hadn't felt this good in months.

Suddenly, he woke up and realized he had been dreaming. He felt refreshed and full of positive energy. This was a feeling he wanted to have often, so he resolved to incorporate exercise into his daily routine.

* * *

Only one day had passed since he had started exercising and listening to the CDs, and he already felt much better. He felt that he could conquer anxiety and depression. He further resolved to focus his energy on listening to and following the anxiety program as well as exercising daily.

Week by week, he religiously followed both programs. His exercise schedule was about forty-five minutes per day alternating days between cardiovascular exercise and weight training. It was hard at first to follow the schedule and also to fight through the initial pain his body felt, not having been accustomed to exercise, but it felt good to see his body shaping into something more desirable. The positive energy that flowed through his body and mind after the workouts was even better.

The anxiety program was even harder for him. When he first started, he thought he would just listen to the program and it would magically heal him. He expected to feel like he did during his first relaxation session. It didn't take him long to realize that it was much more work than that.

Some of the CDs had groups of people talking about their struggles with anxiety and how learning certain skills and unlearning certain behaviors had helped them. Controlling negative thoughts, not putting so much pressure on oneself to be perfect, eating right, and figuring out the history and causes of one's anxiety and depression had been important too.

Through the program, he learned to realize that most of his problems stemmed from his pattern of negative thinking. If he looked objectively at himself when he had severe anxiety, he could trace his panic attacks back to an initial negative thought. That thought would often go unchecked and create another negative thought and so on until he was in a frenzied state of panic. The amazing thing was that his body reacted by going into fight-or-flight mode. He learned that the body reacted to what the brain told it to do. Therefore, when he was having a panic attack, it was just his body trying to escape from the situation he had created in his mind.

By the end of the anxiety program, he felt he had come a long way. He hadn't had a full-blown panic attack for nearly three months, and when the anxious thoughts came, he could recognize them and start mentally talking himself out of panic and into a better state of mind. This wasn't enough for him though. He wanted to get to a point where the negative thoughts that plagued him were completely gone and he didn't have to fight them on an hourly basis. The anxiety program was good, but he needed more. He turned to the Internet and started searching for books on controlling one's thoughts. He knew that thought control was the key to controlling anxiety, and he wanted to become an expert in it.

Excitement rushed through him as he found many more books than he had imagined existed on learning to think positively. Some of the quotes posted online from the books resonated within him. Through the website, www.thoughtsalive.com he obtained a great book called "As a Man Thinketh" written by James Allen. It contained some very valuable quotes like: "A man is literally what he thinks"; "Circumstances reveal to a man his true character"; "Put away all selfish thoughts and be free." As he read the quotes and ordered the books, he realized that he had been very ungrateful and self-centered in his thinking. There was so much to learn still, and he found he was as excited as a child on the first day of school to become an expert in thought control.

Hours went by before he felt he had purchased enough resources to help him reach that goal.

Once he received the books, he devoured them one after the other. Soon, he began to believe in himself. He began to believe that he could have a normal life. For him, that meant having a good job that he loved and was successful at, traveling and enjoying the world, and having a family and a healthy relationship with a beautiful woman.

Could he really do that? Even after all his past broken relationships and the way he had treated so many women in the past? He believed he could, with the help of God. He offered a silent prayer asking God for guidance and help to achieve that goal. Then, he did something that he had learned he should do from some of the books he had read.

Reaching under his desk, he pulled out a large piece of cardboard. Next, he went through magazines and started cutting out pictures that represented the way he wanted his life to look in the future and pasting them on the board. The reason for doing this, according to what he had read, was because the mind takes a mental picture of the image and then it goes down into the subconscious mind.

Soon the board was filled with pictures of planes flying around the world, a six-figure income, healthy people with nice bodies, musicians playing guitars, and one picture that stood out above the rest: a husband, wife, and children.

Feeling a sense of accomplishment and hope for the future, he stood up from his desk. He looked up and saw something that caused him to shudder inside. All good feelings and positive energy left him.

10
THE PICTURE

In the picture, a young woman was sitting on a chair holding a little baby and smiling widely. Both baby and mother looked content. Michael glared at the picture. He couldn't put his finger on why it bothered him so much, but every time he looked at it, he felt anger and fear followed by guilt.

He was angry because in his mind that person had caused him so much pain and suffering; he felt guilty because he believed he shouldn't feel that way towards the woman in the picture.

It was a picture of him and his mother. His sister had given it to him after he and their mother had started talking again a few years earlier. Michael and his mother had shared many feelings from the past and had resolved certain concerns—at least on the surface. However, something deep inside of him caused him to still feel distant and even angry toward her. Despite her attempts to try to fix things from the past, he still felt an inner conflict when thinking about her.

In order to try to force himself to get over his feelings toward her, he had put the picture up in his room. He thought that if he looked at the picture enough times, he could overcome feelings from the past, but the more he looked at the picture, the sicker he became.

"I should want a picture of my mother up," he told himself.

Suddenly, in his mind, he replayed the last conversation he'd had with his mother before their estrangement. He was almost a twelve year old boy and he had decided he wanted to live with his father. His mother was adamant that he not live with his father. However, in his young mind, everything that his mother had told him about his father was a lie and he felt betrayed by her. Furthermore, he felt more at peace visiting his father and stepmother than he had with anyone since his own parents' divorce.

His mind went back even further to when he was living with his mother at the age of nine. He could picture himself as a scared and angry young boy, angry at his father and at the world. Life wasn't fair, and he was out to destroy anything in his way. He pictured the kids he had bullied in school and the teachers he had been belligerent toward, and then his mind went back to another instant.

It was dark, and his friends were gathered together. His friend had stolen some alcohol from his parents and they all decided to try it. Soon, the whole neighborhood could hear the sirens, and cop cars were arriving at the scene...

Although he was young, he was already getting in trouble with the law, and he felt bad inside. His soul was suffering, and he wanted a new life. He had tried reasoning with his mother, but she didn't understand. Angry words were exchanged, and tempers flared. She ended up telling him she never wanted to talk with him again, which stopped him in his tracks.

Not only had she betrayed him by telling him things about his father that weren't true, but she had now disowned him. He could picture himself as a young boy with his head in his hands crying because he had just received the ultimate rejection. In that moment, his heart hardened toward his mother. Things would never be the same.

Michael looked again at the picture, and a well of emotions including sad feelings of frustration followed. Although she had since apologized, part of him wanted just to forget about his mother as if she didn't exist. She didn't exist as he had known her. The only connection he felt was on a superficially amicable basis, but he didn't trust her at all. In fact, he didn't really trust women in general. Seeing this picture just reminded him of the string of broken relationships he had racked up over the course of time.

Sitting back in his chair, he started thinking about all the women he had dated over the years. He had been out with more than he could count, and just when things seemed to be progressing well, he would start to panic. He remembered that happening on more than one occasion when they would talk to him about committing to a more serious relationship. His mind would race back to events of his childhood and his mother, and he would start to panic inside. Usually, the woman would wonder what she had said or done, but he was too embarrassed to say anything. In most cases, he would then make excuses and quit seeing her, leaving her confused and wondering if there was something wrong with her.

He knew deep down that it wasn't her fault. It was his. What was wrong with him?

As he lifted the picture and tucked it away in the back of his closet; he whispered a silent prayer for guidance. His prayer would be answered very shortly.

11

BEAUTIFUL BLESSING

"Um…hi, Michael," a soft, feminine voice said from behind him.

Somewhat startled, Michael quickly turned around and looked down at a woman he had seen but never really spoken with before. She was short and petite and had long black hair that flowed to the middle of her back. He remembered a few times seeing her in mixed company and quickly tried to think of some common ground they might have. Sensing his slight confusion, she spoke again.

"The strangest thing happened the other day. While I was praying, I had a distinct feeling that I should talk with you," she said. "I think we should meet sometime this week."

This was something that Michael didn't hear every day. In fact, he couldn't remember this ever happening. It was all so sudden. He didn't have time to really think about it.

"Sure," he said trying not to sound too skeptical. "Where you wanna meet?"

They decided to meet at a park close to the waterfront.

Although the encounter was a bit strange, there was something about the way she was so determined and fervent about meeting with him—almost as if she were on a mission. Michael was curious about this and was interested in what she had to say. He racked his mind for a few moments, trying to remember her name, and finally, it came. She was Japanese, and her name was Emi, which meant "beautiful blessing." Little did Michael know how much of a blessing Emi would be.

* * *

Sunlight glimmered through the trees and spread out onto the water, which shimmered below. Michael watched as the waves carried the light gently to the shore and placed it on the beach's surface to warm the tiny crabs playing between the small rocks. He closed his eyes and breathed in the ocean air.

His eyes popped open abruptly when he heard a voice.

"Am I interrupting something?"

He turned to see Emi walking briskly toward him, hair bouncing and a slight smile on her lips.

"Uh…no," he said, "just enjoying the good day."

She sat down next to him and looked out across the water at a sailboat.

"It's amazing how much energy and power water has." She was getting philosophical already. "When controlled, it can be a very useful and essential force in our lives for all kinds of things, such as transportation, cleaning, survival, even generating energy. But if it is uncontrolled, it can wipe out a whole city."

The imagery was effective. Michael thought about all the boats, from the tiniest canoe to the large barge he saw in the water in front of him. The water was powerful enough to carry all sizes of boats. He thought of the large reservoirs he had seen and the dams that generated huge amounts of electricity. Then his thoughts turned to the recent flooding that had been going on in a city just south of where he lived. He could still feel the aching in his arms from lifting the sand bags he had volunteered with his church to fill and place in an effort to thwart the water threatening to wipe out the lower-lying parts of town.

His thoughts were interrupted again.

"You know," said Emi, "water is a lot like our thoughts."

Michael stopped and looked at her. How did she know he had been reading about thought control recently? Why was she already prying into the details of his life? What made her think he would trust her and open right up to a stranger like that?

Amid all the questions, he started to reflect on what she had said. He remembered hearing in the past that water would follow the path of least resistance and would flood if it didn't have borders to guide it. The same thing applied to the negative thought patterns he had developed over the years. He had allowed them to go unchecked and run rampant, eventually leading to severe anxiety and panic attacks, followed by depression. He pictured other times in his life though, when he had channeled his thoughts in a positive direction. Most recently, he pictured himself up on the stage receiving his graduate degree.

He sensed she knew she had hit a chord within him and didn't want to appear so obvious, so he stopped thinking and turned to her.

"So what makes you say that?" he said.

"God," she said. "God sent me to you, and I have a feeling what I have to share is essential for your life."

Normally, that statement would have freaked Michael out. He would have chalked her up as one of those weirdos always claiming to have visions about the Second Coming of Jesus happening the next day and telling everyone to head to the hills and wait for the earth's destruction. However, the recent prayer he had prayed came to his mind, and he had learned in life that prayers are usually answered through other people.

"Well, thank you for listening to God," he said. "What do you feel God is telling you to tell me?"

Emi went on to describe how she had received a feeling that he was suffering internally. She didn't know what he was suffering from or why, but she did sense that his internal energy was off. While she was talking, Michael noticed she used that word a lot—*energy*.

"You use the word *energy* a lot," he said. "What do you mean by that?"

"I thought you'd never ask!" Emi said. She adjusted her position on the beach and turned toward Michael. She leaned slightly forward, preparing to use her hands in her explanation.

"You see," she began, "our bodies are energy sources and have several energy points called chakras."

Using her hands, she pointed to various parts of her body. "We have one here, here, here, and here. When our thoughts or emotions are left unchecked, it can throw off the balance of our internal chi and we become unhealthy, either emotionally, mentally, spiritually, physically, or in severe cases, a combination of some or all of them."

Michael reflected on that statement. He definitely felt he was unhealthy in many areas and had experienced how emotional and mental imbalance had manifested itself physically in the form of panic attacks and depression. He was certainly intrigued and wanted to find out where she was going with all of this.

She could tell, so she got right to the point.

"I think you should come to our clinic," she said looking at him earnestly. "You won't have to pay because I am an apprentice and need the clinical hours."

Michael was wondering what she could be referring to. Was she a nurse? A doctor? A psychologist?

Again, Emi proved she had a knack for reading people and reached out to him, touching him gently on the arm to assure him he didn't need to worry.

"I work under a lady who practices Reiki."

12

LIFE ENERGY

"Reiki?" Michael wondered out loud. "What is that?"

He didn't want to sound rude, but things were getting strange.

Emi explained, "It is a Japanese word that is very hard to translate. *Rei*, on a deep level, means the life source for all living things on the planet. In Western cultures, we say *God*. *Ki* means energy source. Our bodies are made up of various sources of energy. When we have negative thoughts that flow through our bodies, they cause disease. As a Reiki therapist, we can sense negative energy and help remove it and replace it with good energy."

Michael was curious. He had tried going the traditional route with the psychologists and doctors and knew he couldn't just will away his negative thoughts and his even deeper negativity toward his mother, which was affecting him emotionally. He thought about his options and decided to give it a try. Besides, it was free.

"So when do you wanna start?" he asked decisively and looked up.

"How about this week?" Emi replied.

* * *

Water gently and soothingly trickled over a glistening rock into a shallow pool below. Soft sounds permeated throughout to create an ambiance of serenity. Candles provided a soothing scent as their lights danced delicately along the wall and up to the ceiling.

Michael lay still underneath a blanket as Emi and Kigo, the head Reiki specialist, moved their hands about three to four inches away from his body. They had explained before the session how our bodies emit energy, and that through this process, they would be able to identify both positive and negative energy and potentially the sources from which the energy came.

A flicker caught Michael's eye as he glanced upward to the ceiling. The flame seemed to be moving in sync with the music. Mesmerized, he kept his eyes on the flame and soon drifted off into a deep slumber.

Something was warming his face. He blinked and looked up to see a ray of sun streaming down through the thin and wispy clouds. The sound of waves gently lapping grabbed his attention, and he lifted himself up off the sandy beach. Dusting the sand from himself, he stretched to see the most beautiful sandy white beach he had ever seen. It seemed to go on for miles. Walking toward the water, he noticed that it was crystal clear. He could see tropical fish swimming playfully near the water's edge as he walked into the lukewarm ocean.

Suddenly, something caught his eye, and he turned to see a huge sea turtle climbing up out of the water and onto the beach. As he started walking toward the turtle, he noticed something that he somehow hadn't before. Although the beach was long and wide, he was the only one there.

The turtle lost his attention.

This is strange, he thought and looked everywhere for a trace of human existence.

Although it seemed a bit eerie that no one else was there, he felt so relaxed just listening to the water and the waves that he went back onto the beach and lay down, closing his eyes. The warm sun from above and the heated sand from below wrapped him into a state of contentment.

Just as he was closing his eyes, he thought he heard something.

"Michael," the voice seemed to say.

He didn't open his eyes, as he thought it was just a sound from the wave.

"Michael!" The voice sounded very familiar.

"Michael!" The voice was not only familiar but full of love and kindness that warmed him like the sand and sun.

He lifted himself up a bit and looked down the beach to see something that sent a thrill of excitement down his spine.

It was a beautiful woman walking down the beach. Her perfect form filled out the swimsuit she was wearing, and he was entranced by how familiar and beautiful she appeared. As she came closer, he noticed that she was the only woman he had ever truly loved. It was Mei!

He jumped up and started running to her. She picked up her pace, running toward him as well. Although they were in close proximity, he thought it was odd that she kept reaching out to him, calling his name.

They were within an arm's length of each other now.

He could hardly contain himself. He wanted to reach out and imagined how good it would feel to hold her body close to his again with the warm sun hitting them as the waves lapped gently along the shore.

He reached out to her, and just as they were about to embrace, he heard it again.

"Michael!" his eyes popped open, and he looked up from the table to see Emi and Kigo smiling at him.

"You were very relaxed, which is a good thing. Welcome back!" Kigo said as she handed him a drink.

"Drink this green tea; it will replenish your energy. We'll be waiting outside and can give you an assessment of what we discovered."

* * *

"So what did you find out?" Michael asked matter-of-factly as he sipped the cold green tea. He looked down at it. It tasted kind of like grass, but if they said it would help, he was fine with drinking it.

"Well…we discovered a lot," said Kigo. Judging by the way she said it, Michael knew he should sit down because it was going to take awhile.

Kigo went on to remind Michael that they measured the chakras in his body, which indicated the level of energy, positive and nega- tive, that he had. Each chakra represented something different as it pertained to various aspects in his overall well-being. Everything was fine until she got around to one of the final chakras.

"I'm very concerned about this certain chakra," Kigo said. "Do you have some unresolved issues from past relationships in your life? I mean with people very close to you?"

Michael couldn't keep the amazement, shock, and slight fear from his eyes as he looked up at her and said, "Um…yeah, I do."

How did she know about that? Had he talked in his sleep? He hadn't explained his concerns about his mother or the anxiety and depression struggles with either Emi or Kigo intentionally. Yet, somehow, Kigo could read him almost like a book.

"Tell me what you have been struggling with," Kigo urged. "We can help you get back on the right track and gain positive energy in your life."

Michael was starting to believe in what they were doing. For the first time, he felt like a practitioner was working on healing the root causes of his struggles rather than just masking the symptoms. Therefore, he decided to tell it all.

For the next half hour, he described his early childhood with his parents fighting and creating an unstable home environment. He described the feelings of abandonment he had had when his mother told him she didn't want to see him again. When he talked about the anxiety and depression problems that had come up most recently, he realized that although he had learned how to cope with them, they were not resolved.

After he described everything, he sat back in his chair, somewhat exhausted, as if he had just worked out. It felt good to get all that off his chest and share it with someone who was at least trying to resolve the issue instead of hide it.

Kigo then looked Michael earnestly in the eye and said, "We can help you, but you will have to commit. It will take hope and effort on both of our parts, and at times, it may become difficult for you." She then leaned forward in her chair and said, "Are you ready to commit?"

Michael wanted more than anything to be free of his inner struggles and was willing to do anything as long as it didn't include taking drugs.

"Yes!" he said resolutely. "I'm willing to do anything it takes."

"Good!" said Kigo, as she leaned back in her chair. "Emi, tell him what his next steps are. Michael, I look forward to seeing your progress." And with that said, she left the room.

Emi looked up at Michael and gave a slight smile. "I had a feeling this would be a good thing," she said. "You will need to make weekly visits for an hour at a time. What day of the week is best for you?"

* * *

As Michael shut the door of the clinic behind him and breathed in the fresh air, he noticed that for the first time in a long time, he felt completely peaceful and confident. He was excited about trying a new approach to healing that didn't include pills and potions and that would get to the root cause of his issues. With a pronounced bounce in his step, he walked toward his car and turned on the radio. A song by Collective Soul was playing that fit perfectly with the way he felt. "Oh, I'm feeling better now!"

He sang the song loudly as he drove away.

13

THE CAMPFIRE

The sound of trickling water falling gently into a quiet brook filled the air. Michael gently closed his eyes and breathed in the pleasant and relaxing scent being emitted from the candles.

He had been going weekly for a couple months now. Each time, he would feel so energized and full of positivity, but over the course of a few days, negative thoughts and old familiar feelings of failure and bitterness would creep back, eventually pushing him toward the anxious tendencies he was trying to overcome.

The door opened quietly, and Kigo entered the room.

"Here, drink this," she said and handed him some of the standard green tea.

Michael listened as Kigo spoke with a deeper intent and meaning than she usually did.

"I've been thinking a lot about you for the past few weeks," she said. "Each week, you come back with the same core imbalance in your chakra that deals with relationships."

Michael thought back on his failed relationships with women, friends, and ultimately his own mother.

Kigo could tell Michael was digesting her words and seized the opportunity. "I want to try something new with you today," she said. "I want to try something called neurolinguistic programming, or NLP."

Michael hadn't heard of it before, but he was up for anything except for taking drugs.

Kigo continued, "Some people compare NLP to hypnosis, but it is not really hypnosis. It is a reprogramming of one's thought patterns. The way it works is to have the patient get into a very relaxed state. The practitioner then asks questions to pull up images, and the patient describes what he sees and tries dealing with the problem. How would you feel about doing this today?"

Michael was eager to try anything that might help, so he agreed. Soon, he was lying down with his eyes shut. Kigo was talking, and images were coming into his mind.

* * *

A large campfire snapped and crackled on a sandy beach as the nearby ocean waves fell distinctly in the outskirts of the fire's glow. People started gathering around the fire.

Michael looked around and saw one of the figures was his father, another was his mother, and a third was him, but much younger. This Michael was eleven years old.

His father beckoned the young Michael to come closer to him and stand by the fire. Young Michael did so without any hesitation. When his father told him he needed to go visit his mother on the other side of the fire, he became very hostile and wouldn't move an inch. Why would someone who said she didn't want to see him all of a sudden want to be friendly with him, let alone be able to provide comfort? He glared at her from across the fire and turned his head.

Despite doing all he could to help his son, Michael's father couldn't get him to go to his mother. He looked up at the thirty-year-old Michael with eyes that seemed to say, "Please help him."

"Michael!" Michael said as young Michael turned and looked up at the older version of himself.

"What happened to your hair?" said the young Michael, "It's all gone!"

"Be careful what you say there, Michael!" older Michael warned. "This will be you someday! Come on over here. Let's have a chat."

Young Michael liked the older version of himself and trusted him, so he left the fire and walked over to him.

"I can see you don't want to hug your mom or get anywhere near her," said older Michael. "Why is that?"

Clearly, the older version of Michael was delusional if he was encouraging a conversation with his mom, young Michael thought as he trudged through the heavy sand toward the older Michael.

Once young Michael had arrived just outside of the warmth of the fire, old Michael put his arms around him and looked ahead. His mother was still standing close to the fire looking alone and a bit sad.

"Why don't you want to go to your mom?" asked older Michael.

Young Michael quickly replied, "She doesn't care for me. What mother leaves her kid? I thought she loved me, but she doesn't. I actually hate her!"

The older version of Michael knelt down in the sand and got to eye level with young Michael.

"Do you trust me?" he asked young Michael.

"Yes, I completely trust you."

"Good. Then listen closely to what I tell you," older Michael firmly responded. "Now that I'm an adult, I can see that our mother said what she said and did what she did because of all the stress that was in her life at that time. Although she shouldn't have said and done those things, she was under a lot of pressure, going through a divorce, struggling with finances, dealing with depression, and trying to raise four kids alone."

Young Michael trusted the older version of himself, and for the first time, he started seeing things from another perspective besides his own.

The older version of Michael saw his words were sinking in, so he continued, "Look at me. I am you twenty years from now. You must forgive your mother, or else I can't move on. I've been hurting other people because of the bitterness left deep inside, and only you can help me resolve it. For us to have the life we want, please forgive your mother."

The words registered with young Michael. He could see he wasn't hurting anyone but himself by not forgiving his mother. Plus, he realized that she was suffering greatly as well. He turned and started walking toward the fire and toward his mother.

Young Michael nervously looked up as his mother looked down. With tears in her eyes, she apologized for what she had done and said to him, not realizing the impact they would have. A feeling of complete release and freedom swept over him as he looked up at her and told her he forgave her, and they embraced by the campfire with tears flowing freely.

Young Michael glanced out to see the older Michael smile approvingly and turn and walk away into the shadows.

* * *

"Wow! You did a great job!" exclaimed Kigo as she helped Michael up into a sitting position. She handed him another green tea to drink.

"Seriously, I have never seen someone progress so well in the first NLP session. You did so well that I think you won't really have to have another NLP session. In the session, as I talked and you brought up those images from the past, your subconscious mind dealt with the issues that have been holding you back, which mainly were related to not forgiving your mother. Throughout your life, you've subconsciously been in pain and fear and have acted out toward women accordingly. You will see a great change in your life from here on out," declared Kigo.

As Michael left the session, he definitely felt better than he ever had before. Although he felt optimistic about his circumstances, he didn't know how things would play out. He just had faith everything would continue improving.

14
THE PROPOSAL

The numbers were looking back at him like an enemy daring him to come even one step closer. This time around though, it was an enemy that he had faced many times before: fear. Michael was staring at the phone wondering if he should make the call. It had been over a year since he had been on a date with any women and nearly two years since he had ended his relationship with Mei.

He thought about the last time he had seen Mei, just over a week ago.

They were both vacationing at the same resort and had run into each other. She had walked up to him through the crowd, and he was as awestruck as he had been the first time they met. The friends who were with him and had heard about her called him crazy for ending a relationship with such a beautiful woman.

* * *

As she walked up to him, her beautiful eyes, the image of which had been seared into his memory, glanced up at him, his heart skipped a beat like it always did before. He felt his face flush and turned away, forcing himself to shut off any thoughts or ideas of getting back together with her, or even associating with her. But he couldn't pull himself away from the attraction he felt toward her.

He spent that whole weekend with her. Although there were other people around, they seemed drawn to each other in every situation.

One day, they both decided to go and explore in the frozen wilderness. They found a huge lake and ran out onto its frozen surface, slipping and sliding as they pretended they were ice skaters. Playfully throwing snowballs and slipping around, they became very cold and returned to the lodge for some hot chocolate and a movie. During the movie, Mei laid her head on Michael's lap and fell asleep as he gently stroked her hair.

The next day, while all their friends played games, they stayed in a different room and just talked for a few hours.

When the trip was over, Michael felt completely sure that she was the girl he wanted to pursue. Never before had he felt that way toward anyone, and even after the years apart, he still felt the same way toward her. Although they hadn't discussed getting back together, he felt that he would be missing out on the greatest opportunity in his life if he didn't give it another try.

* * *

That was two weeks earlier, and now he was staring down at the phone going back and forth between making the phone call and walking away.

On one hand, he felt ready for what he was about to do. He had spent the last few months repairing his relationship with his mother and cleansing himself of any form of abusive behavior toward himself and others—especially women. He felt more ready for a real relationship than he ever had before.

However, on the other hand, he was petrified. What if he hurt her again? What if his feelings toward her changed? What if the anxiety and depression battles resurfaced? What if she didn't want him anymore?

While he was holding the phone and debating in his mind, he looked up and saw what he called his "board of dreams." It was the white board covered in cut-out pictures of what he wanted in the future. Among the pictures symbolizing the exotic places he wanted to travel to, the six-figure income he wanted to earn, the music he wanted to create, in the lower left hand corner, was a picture of a family. His thoughts focused on that image.

When he thought about having a beautiful family, he first thought about having a healthy relationship with the woman of his dreams. He pictured a woman who enjoyed many of the same activities he did, had the same values he did, supported him in his goals, struggled with him during challenges, and was his best friend. He also pictured someone who was attractive and had the potential of being a very good mother.

As he thought about what he wanted, his mind went back to Mei. She was nearly perfect in his eyes and matched up with almost everything he wanted. With this in mind, he dialed the number, and it started to ring.

* * *

The part of Michael that was afraid to face rejection breathed a sigh of relief after the phone rang a few times. Maybe she wasn't there! Part of him was afraid to face Mei after everything he had done to hurt her.

However, more of him wanted to share everything he had been working on over the past couple of years with her. She had been the unfortunate recipient of the effects of his major anxiety and depression episodes. Neither of them understood what was going on. But it all made sense to him now, and he wanted to tell her. He wanted to give things another try, especially since he felt healthy.

His thoughts were interrupted.

"Hello?" said Mei. She wasn't sure who it was because she had erased Michael's number from her phone. He had been the only person she had truly loved, and after he had broken up with her for no apparent reason, she was left wondering what she had done wrong. She had wanted closure and understanding at least, but for months, Michael wouldn't talk about it. There was a huge wall that somehow had developed within him, and she couldn't get through. Therefore, she had moved on, blocking any thoughts of him out of her mind.

"Mei!" Michael said humbly. "It's me, Michael. How are you?"

How am I? Mei thought as a flood of emotions swept through her like a tsunami. She felt her heart jump with excitement at hearing his voice. It had been very good to see him for a few days. She had forgotten how much she was drawn to him on so many levels. There had always been something different about him, something that set him apart from all the other guys. He had also always been so respectful toward her.

Then she thought about how it had been dating him and how he had pushed her and pulled her back and forth emotionally for so long. She felt a strong resolve never to let that happen again. At this stage, she wasn't angry with Michael, although she had been for months. She was indifferent toward him. She had to be, to protect herself emotionally. With this in mind, she responded coolly.

"Well, Michael, is there something you need?"

Michael was a man on a mission. He knew what he wanted, and it was Mei. For years, he had been the top salesman in his company; he knew this call was the greatest sales call of his life. He had to convince Mei somehow to come back to him after he had broken her heart and been essentially silent for two years. He decided to go straight into his sales pitch.

"Mei," he said with a tone of admiration as he thought about how lucky he was that she was even listening to him, "I've found out a lot about myself over the past two years. I found out why I pushed you away, and I found out that I was suffering from anxiety and depression as a result of things from my childhood. More than that, I have been working and have learned how to control anxiety and depression."

Mei was intrigued; she was curious about where Michael was going with his comments. She thought back on the time they were at a restaurant and he had abruptly gotten up and run to the bathroom, panic-stricken. Times like those had confused her terribly. On one hand, he was the nicest, kindest, most entertaining guy she had ever met. Even after two years, he was still the standard of what she was looking for in the man she would spend her life with. However, on the other hand, he would suddenly freak out on her and shut down completely. The harder she had tried to help him, the more he closed up. As she remembered those rough times, she was glad to be out of the relationship.

She continued to listen guardedly.

"The other day when we spent time together, I realized something," Michael continued. "I have never enjoyed someone's company like I do yours. You are so smart, beautiful, and fun to be with. I admire your ability to relate to other people and how kind you are. Never before have I been so attracted to someone on so many levels."

Michael paused for a moment as he considered what he was about to propose. He didn't wait long though, because he knew it needed to be said. "I want to give it another try. I'm proposing that you and I get back together."

Mei had been subconsciously aware that this was where Michael was going and was quite flattered. She had dated a few guys over the past couple years, but no one had been as engaging, fun and, yet as spiritual as Michael. She felt the same way he did. But when he said the words, her defenses came right back up.

Although he had been the most exciting guy she'd ever been with, he also required the most maintenance. He was unstable in his commitment and wavered so easily. Just the thought of investing her love and energy back into him caused stress in her soul. There was so much that needed to change for it to work, and she just wasn't sure if it was possible.

It had been about twenty seconds since Michael had made his "offer," and he was now starting to worry. There was still silence on the other end.

Michael's heart sank when he finally heard Mei speak.

15
A NEW APPROACH

"Give me a few days to think about it," she said with an exhausted sigh.

Michael couldn't believe it. He thought she would feel the same way, given that she had seemed to the other day when they had spent so much time together. He believed she had seen the same chemistry between them that he had. It should be a no-brainer that they get back together. He became nervous that he had messed things up beyond repair. Not willing to give up, he spoke.

"I respect that, Mei. I realize that I hurt you in the past, and I'm sorry. I respect you though, so give me a call when you're ready to let me know."

The conversation ended.

Both Mei and Michael felt drained emotionally.

Michael sat and stared at the phone for a long time, deep in thought.

Mei stared at the wall for awhile and then thought that it would be good to hear some objective advice. She decided to go over to her friend Britt's house and talk it over with her.

* * *

"You've gotta get back with him!" Britt said as she clapped her hands and looked up to the sky. "Can't you see how well you connected with him on the trip?"

"Well…yeah," Mei replied hesitantly.

"I know you guys had issues in the past," said Britt, "but you've gotta look past that. How many guys take the time to first admit they have anxiety and depression and then attack the issue?"

"Probably not that many," said Mei.

"You're right! Not that many," said Britt. "I'll tell you what. If you don't go for him, then I will."

Britt said this intentionally to get Mei's competitive juices going, and it worked.

Although Mei felt very hesitant about getting back with Michael, she couldn't bear to think of him with another woman. Plus, something deep down within her felt that this time was different.

"Okay, I'll do it!" said Mei.

On her way back from Britt's house, she called Michael.

* * *

Michael nervously wiped a bead of sweat away as he entered the café and looked around. Mei had called him the day before and without saying much about her decision told him she would like to meet. Part of him was grateful she hadn't turned him down flat. He actually hadn't even thought it would get this far. At first, he had thought she would take him back with open arms. The picture he had of them running toward each other just as they had in the past was now down to a flicker of hope that she would want to see him again.

Looking to his left, he saw her sitting alone and walked toward her. This felt a lot like a business deal to him, but he took comfort in that because he had negotiated and closed many deals in the past. He thought as long as he could keep his eye on the end result of getting her back, he would be willing to do almost anything.

After exchanging pleasantries, Mei and Michael got down to business. Since Mei had been the one to make the arrangements, Michael let her take control of the conversation and just went with the flow. He hoped that she hadn't made him come to this café just to turn him down nicely.

"I did a lot of thinking over the weekend," Mei started.

Michael thought this was a good sign, but then Mei started sharing more of her thoughts and feelings.

"You broke my heart, Michael. I shut you out and closed you out of my mind and my life for two years. You were nearly dead to me. When we were together, you were so wishy-washy and back and forth. Your problems were too hard for me to deal with. I need some stability. I want a guy who loves me and is willing to do anything for me and not run away."

She paused and looked at Michael, trying to gauge his reaction. He looked rather calm, so she went on. "If we get back together, we're going all the way this time. I think we know each other well enough. We're going to date only each other as if we're heading toward making a life with each other. If you treat me wrong or back out, it's over and there will be no more second or third chances."

She paused again. Michael could see she was more serious than she had ever been before. She was more determined and self-confident than he remembered her. This was a good thing. He was used to girls bending over backward to accommodate him and someone he respected and loved standing up to him was just what he needed.

"Will you be that man for me?" finished Mei.

Thoughts were swirling around inside Michael's head. A small part of him wondered if he could commit to that. He had been ruining relationships for so long and doubting himself repeatedly for so long that he wasn't sure if he could commit. However, he remembered the feelings he had felt with Mei, which he had never felt with any other woman, and he knew he must commit, but also be honest with her.

"Mei," Michael said tenderly, "you are the standard by which I judge all other girls. I didn't realize until we were apart how much you meant to me. When I saw you again on that trip, it all came back to me. I can't promise I won't have anxiety, but I can promise that I will do my best to be the man you deserve."

He then looked her directly in the eyes and reached out for her hand. As their hands interlocked, he said, "Will you have me back?"

She tightened her grip and replied, "Yes, yes, I will. We can work things out together."

16
RESCUE

"I just don't think I can do this anymore!" exclaimed Michael as he buried his head in his hands.

He was visiting Ed, one of his best friends, and discussing the roller-coaster ride that had he had been on emotionally since getting back together with Mei a few months back.

Things went very well for the first couple of weeks after they got back together. Both Mei and Michael were pleasantly surprised at how well things were going. However, after a few weeks, the doubts started creeping into Michael's mind, and he would push her away. Sometimes he would even get agitated with her for trying to help. After he pushed her away and had time to think about things, he would realize what he had done. He would then call her and reel her back in, and the cycle would go on and on.

Even though Michael had suspected that he would still have some lingering anxiety issues surrounding a serious relationship, he had no clue that things would be so difficult. Even though he knew he loved her, frequently, his emotions would shut down and he would push her away if she tried getting too close. Negative thoughts about himself, her, the relationship, and life as a couple in general would paralyze him emotionally and bring him to tears.

Mei did the best she could to help, but she was confused and lost as well. On many occasions, all she could do was hold him in her arms as he cried, both of them feeling completely defeated and exhausted emotionally.

Most recently, they had had an argument that resulted in Mei driving for a few hours to go to her parents. Unbeknownst to him, she was seriously considering ending the relationship with him once and for all.

Michael had decided to drive to Ed's house for some counsel on the matter.

Ed was a good friend for Michael because he would usually listen to him and offer objective advice, if it was solicited. As a general rule, however, he wouldn't share his opinions unless he was asked to do so.

This day was a bit different though. Ed could tell the argument between Michael and Mei had been a big one. He saw how good things were for both Michael and Mei when Michael wasn't having anxiety or depression issues, and he felt he needed to say something. After listening for a long while, Ed decided he had to be bolder than usual.

"Michael," Ed said, "I've known both of you for years now. I can see that she makes you a better person, but you need to see that for yourself. Before you consider just throwing the relationship away, take some time and really think about what you are doing. Do you or do you not want to have a companion in your life? Do you or do you not want a family? If the answer is no, then go ahead and break up with her. If the answer is yes, then be honest with yourself and with me and tell me if you think there is a better girl out there for you."

Ed paused to let his words sink in.

Michael reflected on all the times he had felt so close to Mei and how it hurt him so much not to have her in his life. He knew he had to make a big decision. He was at a proverbial fork in the road, and he had to choose to either be with her or let her go. If he was with her, it was going to have to be all the way. There was no middle ground, which was what he had been trying to dance on.

Michael thought about how he had worked so hard to overcome his issues with forgiving his mother and learning how to deal with anxiety and depression. He thought of all the people who had helped him along the way. He then reflected on the things he had written in his journal of gratitude and how grateful and lucky he felt to have Mei in his life. His thoughts then turned to the board of dreams that included a future with a beautiful wife and children. Happiness flooded through him as he thought about a life with Mei.

Suddenly, something within Michael lit up. He knew what he wanted to do. He thanked Ed for helping him and got into his car to call Mei and let her know what he truly felt toward her.

* * *

Meanwhile, Mei was visiting with her parents. She had felt so sure about giving it another try with Michael, especially after he had gone through all the effort to get his life figured out. Tears streamed down her face as she thought of the time and energy she had invested into the relationship that appeared to be crumbling before her like a brick building in a severe earthquake.

"I think you need to drop him," Mei's mother firmly advised. "He has a lot of potential, but he just doesn't seem to get it."

Mei always valued her parents' input. As hard as it was to hear, she thought her mother was right.

"Unless he can figure out a way to commit and prove he's willing to do so, you're going to continue to be on this roller-coaster ride you've been on for the past few years with him," her mother concluded as she reached over and pulled Mei closer to her.

It was hard for her to see her daughter broken down like this. All she wanted was a good young man who would treat her daughter with the respect and dignity she deserved. Michael just didn't seem to get it at all.

Mei was conflicted. Part of her longed for the good moments she felt when she and Michael were with each other. She reflected on the simple things like looking at the city lights at night while holding each other, cooking together, going out on the town, playing sports together, or listening to him play the guitar while she sang. She noticed a feeling of peace and tenderness overcome her as she reflected on those moments. Then her thoughts turned to the dark times, and her feelings fled like morning dew hit by the sunlight.

She thought of how she had tried to help Michael and how they both watched in horror as he became angry with her for getting too close. She remembered the times when he became too indifferent, or even broke down completely. She thought back to one occasion when Michael lay crumpled on the floor sobbing because his feelings of love toward her had vanished, yet he consciously knew what was happening. He couldn't force his feelings though, and so all she could do was stroke his hair and watch him sob. Her thoughts moved ahead to their most recent dispute, which had led to her driving home to her parents' house.

How could she have a relationship with someone like this?

As much as it hurt her, she realized that unless Michael made some significant changes, showed a higher level of commitment, and overcame his struggles, she wouldn't be able to be in the relationship. She decided she needed to end things with Michael.

A few minutes later, she thanked her mom for the advice and left the house. She knew what her next steps were, and it pained her that she had to do this. She needed to call Michael and end the relationship.

* * *

Just as Michael was getting into his car, brimming with enthusiasm, he glanced down to see that Mei was calling him. He was so determined and excited about what he had to tell her, he hardly noticed the sad tone in her voice.

"Mei!" said Michael enthusiastically. "I'm so glad you called. I was about to call you."

"Oh…really?" said Mei. Michael's tone seemed much more chipper than the last time they had talked. She was taken aback by how upbeat he sounded.

"Before you talk," said Michael, "I just want to tell you something. I had the best conversation with Ed and I came to a realization. I've been sitting on the fence tiptoeing around the issue of committing wholly to you. Sure, I have anxiety and depression issues, but I truly feel that if I commit completely to you, many of my issues would be resolved. I just need to see the obstacle of fear that I have about a serious relationship and tackle it head-on rather than trying to walk around it."

Mei had completely forgotten what she had rehearsed in her mind as to how she was going to break up with him. Michael had never spoken so assuredly about their relationship, and she wanted to see where this was going.

"What I'm trying to say to you is…" Michael paused for a moment. "Well, what if we were to date with the intention of getting married? Think of all the fun times we've had together. Don't you think a life together would be awesome?" said Michael.

"Yes!" she said. The words jumped out before she could even consider holding them back. "Yes, I would love to have a life with you!"

"Then let's talk about it!" said Michael.

17
HAPPY DAYS

Michael looked up at Mei. She radiated so much love and light that he nearly became emotional. She had been there for him through the darkest of times, and now the best of times. She smiled once again as she reached her hand out toward his. They clasped hands, holding them up high as the crowd of family and friends cheered.

Flower petals and rice flew everywhere as they walked down the steps toward their car to leave on their honeymoon. The darkest of days were behind them.

Michael paused and looked at the crowd. His eyes met Emi's and Kigo's in the crowd, and he mouthed a silent "Thank you" to each of them. He scanned the crowd and nodded to friends and family, including Ed and his parents and siblings. They had all been there for him when he needed someone to lean on. Finally, he glanced back at Mei, his beautiful bride, who had persevered with him in the months leading up to the wedding.

Even after they had committed to getting married, Michael had needed to work very hard to overcome his complete fear and anxiety of committing to marriage. There were days when Michael's anxiety and depression was so severe that all Mei could do was hold him in silence as he struggled.

In order to conquer Michael's anxiety and depression, they had worked through anxiety and depression programs together, completed workbooks, worked on dieting and exercise, wrote gratitude journals and made boards of dreams, prayed, and cried together, leaning on God and each other for support. Through it all, Michael had seen the depths of Mei's soul and knew she would be there for him always. Mei knew how determined Michael was to overcome anxiety and depression and had seen his love and willingness to do anything for her too.

As Michael continued to glance across the crowd, he saw his mother. Just a few months before this event, he would have looked at her with indifference and an unforgiving heart remembering what had happened in his early childhood. Now, he looked at her with admiration and respect for what she had gone through. She blew him a kiss, and he knew she meant it. He blew one back at her, realizing once again just how freeing forgiveness was.

He sat down in the car, revved up the engine, and turned on the radio. One of his favorite rock songs, "Shine" by Collective Soul, was playing. The song was fitting, and as they drove away to the lyrics "Heaven let your light shine down!" Michael felt like a touch of heaven's grace had been with him that day. He felt Mei's tender touch.

Part Two:
Twelve Steps to Overcoming Anxiety and Depression without Medication

STEP 1: DESIRE, LABOR, FAITH

The desires we act on determine our changing, our achieving, and our becoming.
—Dallen Oaks

One of my favorite quotes is one from Stephen Covey's famous book *7 Habits of Highly Effective People*. It is simple, yet profound: "Begin with the end in mind."

Many people who struggle with anxiety and depression are overwhelmed and don't even know where to start. However, if you have a deep desire and set the goal to be free of anxiety, it can be accomplished. The individual must first create a vision of what life will be like when he or she is anxiety and depression free.

Think about your own life. Was there anything you accomplished that you didn't first have a desire for? Think about the athlete who wins a race, the artist who finishes a painting, the successful businessman, and the list goes on. I know that in my life, everything I have achieved started with a desire followed by action toward the desired goal.

When I discovered I had depression, I was crushed both physically and emotionally. I had always considered those with depression to be weak. I thought I should just "buck up" and look on the positive side of things. However, I couldn't shake the negative thoughts or prevent the downward spiral I felt I was taking on a daily basis. After a few days of feeling sorry for myself, I came to the conclusion that I had two choices: to continue to feel sorry for myself and essentially do nothing (and possibly get worse), or to put all my energy into reaching my goal of overcoming depression and anxiety.

I decided that I wanted a life without anxiety or depression. I desired with all my heart to overcome it and was willing to work toward that goal. I firmly believed the words of W. Clement Stone: "Whatever the mind of man can conceive and believe; it can achieve…" Once I had firmly planted the seed of desire in my heart, I set the desire in motion by working toward the goal of overcoming anxiety and depression.

I had a hard time picturing what life would look like without anxiety and depression, but I had a tiny seed of hope that I could get there. I had images of how I once was—confident, fun, and a person people wanted around them. When I compared who I truly wanted to be to what I was at that point, it was discouraging, but motivating as well. I began to believe that I could actually do it. I took that little glimmer of hope and planted it firmly in my heart and mind.

I've heard it said that faith is desire plus action. The action I took will be outlined in the ensuing chapters of this book. It was much more difficult than I had originally imagined. Much like the person who begins a marathon for the first time, I didn't know what additional challenges and setbacks there would be along the way. However, with persistence, a vision of life without anxiety and depression, and help from God, I was able to make the journey and complete the race. I overcame anxiety and depression.

LEARNING ACTIVITY

Take a moment now and reflect on your desires. Perhaps it is learning to cope with depression or anxiety; perhaps it is to overcome it completely. Maybe you have other goals as well, such as buying a nice house, going on vacation, achieving personal growth in other areas, etc. As you consider your innermost desires, write down all those that come to your mind. Think spiritually, emotionally, mentally, and physically.

Once you have done this, look at each one again and picture your life in the future after you have obtained that goal. Remove all negative thoughts as they creep in saying, "You can't do this!" Just take some time to focus on how life will be when you have achieved your goal.

Finally, make a visual picture of the goals and desires you have outlined. What worked for me was getting a large poster board and then going through newspapers and magazines cutting out pictures that represented my desires and goals. I then pasted them on the poster board and hung it in my office. You can do the same thing, or if you are an artist, draw the pictures. The point of this exercise is to bring to the surface your goals and put an image in your mind of how you will look and feel when you are anxiety and depression free. Believe me; it is very powerful to have the visual desires in front of you.

STEP 2: PRAYER

Prayer is the soul's sincere desire.
—James Montgomery

The moment I discovered I was struggling with depression, I was devastated. I felt crushed, but I had reached the end of the road psychologically, physically, and internally trying to run from the feelings I was struggling with. I firmly believed in the biblical scripture where Jesus said, "Come unto me all ye that are heavy laden and I will give you rest" (Matthew 11:28). I prayed continuously for strength, guidance, and rest. My mind was sometimes consumed with negative thoughts that would escalate and spin around in my head until I had panic attacks. I would then sink into depression and be angry at myself for allowing myself to be that way.

My prayer was that I could overcome anxiety and depression. I wanted to flip the switch, so to speak, and remove the struggle immediately. However, I also knew from experience and from scripture (i.e., "Your will be done" (Matthew 6:13)) that God allows us to struggle and suffer sometimes to strengthen our faith in Him as well as to help us grow personally. Therefore, my prayer turned to praying for His will to be done and for Him to guide me in the right direction.

From the earliest moment continuing throughout my experience with anxiety and depression, I prayed. I prayed in a variety of ways. Sometimes, it would be out loud while I was driving or out and about. Other times, it was silently in my mind while I was in public. Often, I would pray first thing in the morning and last thing at night. When I prayed, I spoke with God as I would another person. I prayed that I could become the person He wanted me to be: confident, humble, unselfish, and all of the things I felt I wasn't at the time.

Not only did I pray for myself; I had others praying for me. Depending on how close I was with them, I told people of my struggles and asked for specific prayers to be said. I had friends and family who contacted their friends and family asking them to offer prayers on my behalf. There were many prayers being offered.

I continued to pray and struggle over the course of a few years and involved others often. I definitely felt the hand of God reach down and make my burden lighter, as He promises He will do.

When I was totally down and discouraged, he lifted me up in many ways, usually through other people. One day, I was driving my car when negative thoughts came and depression hit; the question of whether it was easier just to die came into my mind. I felt darkness surround me, and I said a silent prayer. Within minutes, my grandfather called me, which was something he seldom did. He said he felt guided to contact me and asked if anything was wrong. I told him of my struggle with depression, and he empathized with me. He shared how he had gone through depression after my grandmother's death and how he overcame it. He gave me the hope that day to keep trying.

Another day, I was in my apartment visiting with a friend. She had struggled with anxiety and depression too. She stopped me as I was talking and told me of her experience and of the Midwest Center for Stress and Anxiety/Depression program (which I discuss later). This proved to be a very good tool in helping me step closer to overcoming anxiety and depression.

On another occasion, I had gotten a prescription for depression and ordered the drug (I think it was Zoloft). As I was taking the medication the first day, I felt very strongly that it was not the right thing for me to do. (Keep in mind, I am not saying my approach is right for everyone. If you are on drugs for anxiety/depression, that is okay. However, I felt guided that it was not right for me.)

Usually, praying on a daily basis gave me the hope and strength I needed to make it through the next hour, day, week, and month. As I continued praying, I felt God leading me step-by-step toward gaining more knowledge of how to overcome anxiety and depression.

LEARNING ACTIVITY

Find a very relaxing, peaceful place where no one will disturb you. Reflect on the greatness of this world and the miracles that surround you. Think of the blessings in your life and also those things that you would like to see improve. If you have not prayed before, use the example Jesus gives for us in the Bible in Matthew 6:13.

Start your prayer by addressing "Our Father in Heaven." Acknowledge His greatness and glory and your weakness, need, and dependence. Ask for His will to be done. Now share your soul with Him. Open up and tell Him of your frustrations, your desires, your dreams, and your goals. Describe how it feels and ask for guidance. Speak out loud as you would to another person and pour out your soul before Him. Next, think of anyone you may have offended and pray for forgiveness. Pray for those who may have offended you, and ask that they be healed as well as yourself, if you still hold bitterness. Close in the name of Jesus Christ.

I promise you that if you do this at least once per day and preferably multiple times per day you will be quietly led through feelings and thoughts or to other people. I promise that God hears your prayers, though He usually does not answer them in ways that we think He will. He answers them in ways that are best for us though. After you offer your prayers, forget about expectations of how He will answer. Simply go on about your day and let things happen. If you do this, it will all work for your own good.

STEP 3: DISCOVER AND DECIDE

Every one of us has in him a continent of undiscovered character. Blessed is he who acts as the Columbus of his own soul.
—Charles L Wallace

When I thought I might be struggling with depression, one of the first things I did was take an online test to determine if I had it. I'm sure there are numerous websites that have similar tests, but the one I used was from the Midwest Center for Stress and Anxiety at www.stresscenter.com. Needless to say, I tested very high in anxiety as well as depression.

Once I had determined that I was suffering from both anxiety and depression, I decided to go the traditional route and see a medical doctor. The solution he offered left something to be desired. I had the goal of finding out root causes for my anxiety, which would trigger panic attacks that would then snowball into depression. When I went to the doctor, he asked a few questions, wrote a prescription for Zoloft. He told me to take it for a few weeks and let it get into my system, then return for a follow-up visit. I felt uneasy (as people with anxiety tend to do) about it but thought I would at least give it a try.

When I returned home, I read through the information on the drug packaging, including the possible side effects. I still felt uneasy but decided to try it. I took the drug for about three days, but each time I took it, it felt very wrong, and deep inside, I knew this wasn't the right thing for me.

In the meantime, I had decided to see a psychologist as well through LDS Social Services. One of the main things I learned from them was that overcoming depression and anxiety had a lot to do with learning how to control thoughts. I also ordered the program called *Overcoming Anxiety and Depression* through the Midwest Center for Stress and Anxiety. This program opened up a whole new world to me and helped me feel like I wasn't alone. I learned that whether or not he or she takes a drug, every person suffering from anxiety and depression needs to work on thought control. I decided that if I needed to work and train my thoughts anyway, I didn't want to use drugs if I didn't have to. Since the doctor hadn't urged me to be on Zoloft, I decided to get rid of it. I threw it away and went to work learning how to train my thoughts.

The next two steps occurred concurrently as I continued the self-discovery process. I will start with the Midwest Center, because it was through that program that I learned I had depression and anxiety as well as discovered coping strategies that helped me later on as I continued working toward overcoming them.

STEP 4: SELF-STUDY

Knowing yourself is the beginning of all wisdom.
—Aristotle

One day, I was talking with my friend and his fiancée about the struggles I was having at work, in church, and in life in general. I mentioned goals not being reached and frustrations with myself, etc. My friend's fiancée said to me, "I think you have anxiety and depression." That stopped me in my tracks. Depression was a sign of weakness to me. I had heard of people and seen people within my family suffer from it, but to me, that was a sign that you were not strong enough to pull yourself up by the bootstraps and fight through it. For me, fighting through it meant ignoring it and pushing it aside. I was very stressed though at the time, so I decided to continue listening rather than discard her advice.

She went on to tell me about a program she had gone through herself when she was suffering from anxiety and depression. The best thing was that she hadn't had to use medication to overcome it. That was music to my ears, because I did not want to use medication. Within a few minutes, I was on the website taking the assessment that I previously mentioned (www.stresscenter.com).

It had been twenty minutes or so, and I was looking at the results with my friend and his fiancée. I felt dizzy as thoughts started racing through my head like a whirlwind. I tested very high in anxiety as well as depression. I started to have a panic attack right there on the spot because I was scared of the results and what they meant. Negative thoughts swirled around within me, my heart started racing, and I became even more depressed.

The next day, I tried going to work, but I just sat out in my car; I couldn't go in. Thoughts and negativity surrounded me. First, I had a major panic attack, which spiraled down into depression as I sat in the car crying and hating myself. That day, I turned the car around and went home. I ordered the program from the Midwest Center for Stress and Anxiety called *Attacking Anxiety and Depression* (www. stresscenter.com). I was willing to do anything in order to overcome my struggles with anxiety and depression.

When I received the program a few days later, I eagerly began working through the CDs. The program setup has you listen to other people tell about their struggles with anxiety and depression and then do activities and assignments that help you start to reprogram your thought processes, manage your thinking, and eventually overcome anxiety and depression. Each week focuses on a different strategy, such as understanding the causes of anxiety and depression, learning how to end panic attacks, training your mind to relax and focus on positive things, and learning how to live a "normal" life without panic and depression.

Over the course of the next few weeks, I began a self-discovery process as I listened to the program and did the activities. I learned that I wasn't alone. Although I had never met the people sharing their stories, I felt better knowing it was not just me and that they had overcome anxiety and depression without medication. I also learned techniques for training my body to relax and release the tension that came from anxiety as well as managing depression.

The first night after receiving the program, while listening to the relaxation CD, I fell comfortably asleep for the first time in months, if not years. Usually, I would fall asleep and have restless sleep with thoughts spinning around my head throughout the night. The CD helped me focus on peace and calmness, and I slept long, hard, and deep for the first time in many months. I woke up the next day feeling refreshed.

I continued using the twelve-week program as it recommended: listening to the relaxation CD at least three times per day, listening to the group-session CDs, and working on the activities in the workbook. Sometimes it wasn't very convenient, but I felt it was a very important program and I always found a way to carve out time each day to work on the suggested activities.

Initially, I thought that I would go through the anxiety program and things would just be better all at once after twelve weeks. I was wrong. The program was very beneficial for me in leading me to self-discovery and teaching me techniques to manage anxiety and depression, but I still felt that there were some deep-rooted issues causing my anxiety. I had some work to do in order to get to the root cause of my symptoms of anxiety and depression, and this program couldn't help with that. Although I was not having panic attacks and depressive episodes in general anymore, there was something deeper that was affecting my relationships and self-image. Every time I would get close to a woman and have to commit to a serious relationship, I would panic and shut down emotionally. I would then sabotage the relationship. I still had a lot of digging to do, and as I learned later, it was all in my head.

LEARNING ACTIVITY

Go to the Midwest Center for Stress and Anxiety's website and take the anxiety test. Learn about your own personal struggles with anxiety and depression. Order the program and begin working on managing anxiety and depression.

STEP 5: THOUGHT CONTROL

A man is literally what he thinks, his character being the complete sum of all his thoughts.
—James Allen

Personally, I believe thought control is one of the most important aspects in learning to overcome anxiety and depression. I say "learning" because I came to know that our thoughts shape who we are and how we behave. We can choose to let our thoughts control us, or we can control our thoughts. Our bodies react to the way we think.

For example, when I was struggling with anxiety, I would have certain triggers that caused negative thinking. One was serious relationships with women. When I got serious with a woman, I would get the thought, *What if I get too close to her?* followed by *She'll leave me and my heart will break.* Then I would picture a lonely life without love and get depressed. I ended quite a few relationships very prematurely as a result.

However, when I met the woman I truly wanted to be with and made the decision within myself that I wanted to overcome those negative thoughts, I made every effort to do so. It took years—literally—but it was worth it.

THOUGHT MAPPING

I learned to control my thoughts from books about the power of our thoughts and how they shape who we become. I also spent a lot of time mapping my negative thoughts and remapping them with positive ones, which is illustrated in the ensuing pages.

THOUGHT MAPPING EXERCISE

I learned that my body reacted to my thoughts…both positive and negative. Therefore, when I was having a panic attack, it always was traceable to a string of negative thoughts left unchecked. In order to get the thoughts in check, I did the following exercise.

First, I would think of the original negative thought I had. For example, in relationships, I would think, *I'm getting too close to this girl*. I would then put it into a simple T diagram like the following:

Negative Thought	
I'm getting too close to this girl	

After I wrote down the initial thought, I would think of the next negative thought that came after the first one and write it down. My experience was that one negative thought led to another and another and so on until I spun out of control and into a frenzy in my mind, which in turn led to panic. The diagram below shows how to map negative thought patterns:

Negative Thoughts	
1. I'm getting too close to this girl	
2. She'll leave me if I get too close	
3. I had better use her before she uses me and leaves me	
4. I'll close myself off emotionally and use her.	
5. I don't care about the relationship anymore	

As you can see, negative thoughts keep get progressively worse. If these thoughts go unchecked and continue to be thought over and over again, the person with anxiety begins believing that is who he or she is and acts accordingly. Negative thinking over time damages relationships, destroys health, and damns our progression as humans.

It is critical that we learn how to stop thinking negatively and turn our thoughts in a positive direction.

Just as negative thoughts can create a monster out of us, positive thoughts can have the exact opposite effect. If we learn to train our minds to think positively, then we'll eventually become the person that we dream of becoming. It takes time, effort, and patience though.

When I was struggling with anxiety, I would outline my negative thoughts as I demonstrated previously. After I had outlined the negative thoughts, I would then put positive thoughts in the opposite column and cross out the negative ones as in the following example:

Negative Thoughts	Positive Thoughts
● ~~I'm getting too close to this girl~~	● The way I feel about this girl is a good thing and I will continue to look for her good qualities
● ~~She'll leave me if I get too close~~	● I choose not to worry about if she'll leave. I will focus on treating her with respect and honor.
● ~~I had better use her before she uses me and leaves me~~	● I choose to treat her with the utmost respect and better than any other guy ever has
● ~~I'll close myself off emotionally and use her.~~	● I will be open and honest in my communication with her publicly and privately.
● ~~I don't care about the relationship anymore~~	● I care about how I treat her because she is an amazing human being that deserves respect.

Although I used one specific example of negative thinking, you can insert any negative thought in and counter it with a positive one. Once I had a negative thought, I would stop, write it down, and focus on the positive thought. I found it helpful to carry a notepad around with me and do this exercise immediately after I had a negative thought.

VISION BOARD

Another activity I found very helpful in channeling my internal thoughts to be more positive and less destructive was creating what I call a "vision board." The concept came from similar ideas I read about in several sources, including Leslie Householder's books (see the appendix for more information).

The way I created my vision board was pretty basic. First, I listed my deepest desires in life. While doing this, I was honest with myself and wrote down the things that I was excited to think about. My list included: overcoming anxiety and depression, marrying the girl of my dreams and having a family, making a six-figure income, having a job that gave me the ability to make my own schedule and travel, staying athletic and physically fit, having enough money to help those in need, and saving for the future.

The next step I took was to find pictures online or in magazines that represented each of those goals.

I then cut out the pictures and pasted them on a white board, which I put up in my room.

Every day, I would spend some time picturing how life would be once I reached my goals. Little by little, I started truly believing that I could indeed reach my goals and I also started believing the person represented by that board was who I truly was. Soon, I had no desire whatsoever to be single and full of anxiety.

It wasn't until a few years after I had been married, we had our beautiful little daughter, and I had received a very significant pay increase that I looked at the board and it dawned on me that everything I had wanted had come to pass.

The key to the process is to realize that it takes time. It isn't a sprint. Rather, it is a marathon. Overcoming anxiety and depression begins within our minds. Over time, my mind became trained to think positively instead of negatively, which in turn led me to overcome anxiety and depression.

As mentioned, some of the books I read were invaluable in helping me learn to control my thoughts. These books, along with specific quotes from them, thoughts I had, and a learning activity are included in the appendix at the end of this book. I highly recommend reading through those because they will help you shape your thoughts in a direction that will allow you to overcome anxiety and depression.

STEP 6: COACH OR MENTOR

To be good is noble, but to show others how to be good is nobler...
—Mark Twain

There are times in life when I can tell I've received a thought and it might be a good idea to act on it. However there are other times, such as the following instance, when I feel that God is telling me to do something. I think many, if not all, of us have felt this at one point or another—we just *know* that we need to do (or not do) something for our protection. One day, as I was driving down the rainy freeways of western Washington, I felt God speak to me through a very distinct thought and feeling. He told me to contact an old friend. I thought that my friend was perhaps in need of help, so I called.

It was good catching up with my friend from a few years before. I learned that she had been busy recording music and had other struggles in life that came with being a single parent but was overall doing very well. Originally, when we started talking again, we shared music we had written and played piano and guitar together. It was fun and refreshing just to let out positive energy through music. As I continued to meet with her on at least a weekly basis, I learned that the reason why I was led to her was not for me to help her, but rather for her to help me.

One day, as we were talking, I shared with her some of my struggles with anxiety and depression and how I was going about dealing with them. At this point, I had learned how to manage things, so I wasn't having full-blown panic attacks, but I was still struggling. One of my greatest struggles was getting into relationships with women and basically using them both emotionally and physically. After I would do this, I would become angry with myself and spiral into depression; I would promise myself I would never do it again but then go back to the bad behavior.

I shared a recent episode with her. She listened to me and then said, "I think you have an addiction that I can help you with." She said it with such confidence that I stopped, intrigued. I wanted to learn more. She went on to pull out a book that was about a program on overcoming sex addiction. While I never had sex with the women I was using, I definitely did struggle with getting too physically and emotionally involved with them. This led to emotional ties that I would subconsciously sever, resulting in anger and frustration for everyone involved. I had been doing this for years, and I couldn't count the number of women I had hurt; it happened over and over again.

She went on to tell me that she had gone through the program herself and had learned how to overcome addictions formed from abandonment and abuse as a child. She went on to explain the program and told me about her experiences as a child and how they had affected her relationships as an adult. As she spoke, it all began to make perfect sense to me. I had felt abandoned as a kid and subconsciously was taking it out on all the women I had dated throughout the years. She went on to describe how she could be my sponsor or I could join one of the sex anonymous groups in the area. I opted to go with her being my sponsor, so we met regularly and started doing the twelve steps.

As we met, I learned that the addiction I had was a large part of the anxiety and depression I felt. One of my deepest desires was to have a loving, functional relationship with a woman, but over the course of the years, I had built a defense mechanism as a result of the abandonment I felt as child. When I would desire a relationship, I would seek out a woman. When I found one, I would experience severe anxiety from the belief that she would use or abandon me, so I would use and abandon her before she had a chance to do it to me. After I had used her, I would beat myself up mentally and sink into depression because I knew it was wrong and I had hurt someone. This cycle had been a pattern for more than ten years and had affected dozens of women.

In addition to going through the twelve-step program during our sessions, I had to eliminate having physical contact with the opposite sex. I decided to focus fully on clearing my mind and loving myself for who I was inside. That meant not dating, which was hard for me.

As I refrained from dating, I focused on rediscovering myself and my relationship with God and others. I wrote songs on my guitar and used that as a sort of therapy during this time as well. I also quit my job and lived off of savings for a few months in order to clear my head and just focus on healing. During this time, I also started doing Reiki, which I will discuss later.

After a few months of working on reshaping and reprogramming myself, I decided to jump back into the "real world" and get a job (mainly because I was running out of money!). I also slowly started taking women out on dates and focused on just treating them with the deepest respect—not getting physically involved but just getting to know them for who they were. This may sound like a small thing for many people, but for me, it was a great step. It helped me with my self-esteem to know I was capable of sincerely treating women with respect.

For me, the greatest evidence of this accomplishment came when I was out of town for a month on a business trip and had met a beautiful young woman. She and I went out a few times per week for a few weeks and became fairly well-acquainted with each other. On the last night, we were hanging out, and as we were talking, she looked me straight in the eyes and sincerely thanked me. She thanked me for being one of the first guys who didn't just look at her physical beauty and try to take advantage of her. She thanked me for getting to know her for who she was and said that she felt the time we spent with each other had blessed her. I felt the same way.

Shortly after this occasion, I became reacquainted with a woman I had always loved but was too scared to pursue a relationship with because of my fear of using her. Historically, I would get close to her and out of fear of using her as I had other women in the past, I would push her away. This time was different for me though. As a result of going through the addiction program, I had confidence that I would treat her with respect. We started dating again and within a few months we were married.

From my experience, having a sponsor help me go through the program was a tremendous benefit for me in overcoming anxiety and depression. When I was too weak to overcome the addiction on my own, it helped to have someone I was accountable to at least on a weekly basis. Over time, I was able to overcome this addiction, and while it didn't completely cure me of anxiety and depression, it did help me gain the confidence and respect for myself that I needed in order to find the root cause of the issues.

Having an official sponsor wasn't the only coach or mentor that helped me. There were many times along the way that I reached out to family members who struggled with depression. Their advice was very good, but most importantly, I felt like I could share my feelings with them without being judged. Speaking with them helped heal me and give me the courage to face another day and I will be forever grateful for those who coached and mentored me.

LEARNING ACTIVITY

If you have formed an addiction that is a result of or a form of trying to "medicate" your anxiety and/or depression, seek help. Confide in a trusted friend, pastor, or other church leader. Many churches have a twelve-step program affiliated with their belief system. If you are not religious, look up an addiction center in your area and seek help.

STEP 7: NLP, REIKI

There is little sense in trying to change external conditions, you must first change inner beliefs, then outer conditions will change accordingly.
—Brian Adams

At church one day, a nice young lady walked up to me and asked me how I was doing. I had only been in group settings a few times with her before, so I wasn't about to get into all the things I was working on concerning anxiety and depression. However, as we started talking, one thing led to another, and she described where she worked and said that she was an understudy of a lady who practiced a Japanese relaxation and healing technique called Reiki. At first, I politely declined the offer, as I still hadn't shared with her the details of my struggles. She insisted that I come though, saying that she had felt guided by God to come to me that day and help me. I could tell she was serious, and since I had been praying for help I agreed to come.

During my first visit, I described my struggles with anxiety, depression, and addictions. After I told her about my situation, the practitioner explained the concept of Reiki to me. Her explanation mirrored that of the International Center for Reiki Training (www.reiki.org): Reiki is a technique that uses the "laying on of hands" to reduce stress and increase life energy. *Rei* means "God's Wisdom" and *Ki* means "life force, or energy." She also went on to describe and demonstrate how our body has chakras, or energy points, that give us our energy. Certain chakras are related to certain aspects of our well-being and if one or many of them are off-balance, we are more likely to feel stress or disease.

After she described everything, it seemed like a good concept, but a bit too New Age and strange for what I was used to. However, I was determined not to take medication to deal with my anxiety and depression, and I felt that I had been guided to this point, so I broadened my perspective and gave it a try. It was one of the best things I did.

I would regularly attend one-hour sessions and meet with both the practitioner/owner and my friend, who was her apprentice. While I was learning to deal with my anxiety issues, I was still holding on to a lot of stress within my body. My muscles were tense frequently, and my mind would still sometimes race. The sessions were a welcome relief from the stress in my head and the world around me.

With each visit, they would ask me how the week had gone and if I felt I was progressing. I would then lie down on a table in a room with dim lighting, quiet music, and usually a soothing little fountain. Next, they would move their hands a few inches above my body on the chakras. They could sense if I was unbalanced internally and use techniques to relax my chakras and release negative energy. After each visit, I felt completely relaxed and as if all negative energy had been released. This went on for a few weeks, and while I didn't feel like it was a total cure for my depression and anxiety, the effects of the visits lasted a day or two and were a welcome relief.

My most memorable, and perhaps important, experience with the "Reiki Lady," as I called her to my friends, was when she asked me about the possibility of using a technique she had studied called Neurolinguistic Programming (NLP). She felt that many of the issues I was dealing with involving stress, anxiety, depression, and certain addictions were a result of unresolved anger I had toward my mother from my childhood. I was open to trying just about anything so I agreed to go along with the new technique.

We started the session as usual with releasing negative energy through the Reiki techniques previously described. After I was relaxed, she started the NLP session.

There are various definitions for and beliefs about NLP. The way I like to view it is that NLP is a way of reprogramming the mind to think or believe something in a different way so as to alter the outward manifestations of that belief. In my situation, I harbored subconscious anger and mistrust toward my mother that was made manifest through my negative self-talk and negative beliefs about the women I became intimate with on any level.

When the NLP session with me began, she asked me to imagine myself, my father, and my mother on a beach with a campfire. She asked me to enter the scene as a thirty-year-old man and look at my-self as a ten-year-old boy. She asked questions about how the thirty-year-old me felt about certain decisions my parents had made and then asked if the ten-year-old me would be willing to let my mother come closer to the fire. The ten-year-old version of me was very bitter, and the only person he trusted was the thirty-year-old me. My NLP practitioner then asked the thirty-year-old me to come and put my arm around the ten-year-old me and explain why my mother might have said what she did or acted a certain way and encourage the ten-year-old to forgive her. By the end of the session, the ten-year-old ver-sion of me was hugging my mother, crying, and forgiving her.

This experience was overwhelming. It was actually a turning point in my healing process in overcoming anxiety, depression, ad-dictions, and abandonment fears. Not long after that session, I was able to completely forgive my mother, which in turn led me to gain confidence in myself and respect for women. It was nothing short of a miracle, and I am grateful that my friend followed her feelings and found me in church that day to lead me to Reiki and NLP.

LEARNING ACTIVITY

Learn about Reiki and see if it is right for you. You can learn about Reiki by doing an Internet search. If you type in "Reiki in (insert your city)," you will probably find practitioners in your area. If you want to educate yourself on Reiki before talking with a practitioner, visit the following sites: www.reiki.org; http://nccam.nih.gov/health/reiki/; or www.reiki.com.

STEP 8: EATING HABITS

One cannot think well, love well, sleep well, if one has not dined well.
—Virginia Woolf

While I was suffering the most with anxiety and depression, I was living in constant fear. Questions ran through my mind, such as: *When would the next panic attack hit and where would it be? Does everyone have these thoughts racing through their heads? Why me?*

I found that in order to help stabilize my thoughts and bring myself into more focus, it was crucial to exercise and eat right, which go hand in hand. If I didn't eat right, I couldn't get a good workout in. If I didn't exercise, I felt down and it was harder to eat right.

There are a multitude of books and plenty of research out there that proclaim the necessity of getting enough exercise and eating right, particularly in relation to overcoming anxiety and depression. The problem that I see most people struggle with is trying to fit it into their schedule and make it a daily routine that sticks. This chapter will describe strategies I applied to work healthy eating habits into my daily schedule.

THE IMPORTANCE OF HEALTHY EATING

I ran triathlons for awhile when I was in my mid-twenties, so I learned the importance of eating lean meat and foods low in saturated fats. I remember after a few months of training and eating lean meats (e.g., fish and chicken), I thought I would indulge myself and eat a big, juicy burger. I hadn't really had anything greasy for months. The burger tasted very good as I ate it, and initially, I felt fine. However, the next morning as I began my training, I felt like there was a rock in my gut and I had to cut my training short because I got so sick from eating the burger. That experience led me to shy away from fatty foods and showed me that it does indeed matter what I put into my body.

Overcoming anxiety and depression is much like training for a race. It is probably the hardest thing I have ever done mentally, and it took me two years to do it. If you are eating foods that do not properly feed the brain and body, you will struggle more in overcoming anxiety and depression. Furthermore, there are some foods that are commonly eaten in our society that actually make anxiety and depression worse.

For example, scholarly journals state that alcohol consumption can lead to depression whereas abstinence can lead to the depression disappearing (Acta Psychiatrica Scandinavica vol. 89 pp. 28-32, Feb, 1994). Other research shows that caffeine can produce anxiety. (Neuropsychopharmacology. 2008, November: 33), and sugar can also lead to anxiety (Journal of Abnormal Psychology. 1986 14(4): 565-577). Coffee, many teas, soda, and many of our processed foods have some or all of these ingredients in them and should be avoided—especially by people who have anxiety and depression struggles.

A good outline for me is found in a scripture called the "Word of Wisdom" in the Doctrine and Covenants (section 89). I use this as a guideline to healthy eating. The "Word of Wisdom" suggests that one not drink alcohol or use tobacco, eat meats sparingly (I recommend eating lean, white meat over fatty red meat), and eat whole grains and lots of fruits and vegetables. It also alludes to the idea that drinking coffee and tea are not good for the body either. In addition to what is outlined in the "Word of Wisdom," I chose to eliminate all soda and caffeine from my diet.

As I followed the guidance of eating plenty of vegetables, fruits, and whole grains and eliminating toxic substances, such as caffeine, alcohol, and fatty foods, I noticed that internally, I felt better. Not only did I feel better, but I could think more clearly and react more quickly.

Some people I talk with about this are concerned because they feel they can't give something up, such as coffee in the morning, a beer after a long day at work, a cigarette to reduce stress, or their sixteen-ounce soda loaded with sugar and caffeine. The fact that they are gripping on tightly to the substance and have a fear of not being able to cope without it is a sure sign that it isn't healthy for the body.

LEARNING ACTIVITY

For those who struggle with anxiety and depression and want to take major strides in overcoming either or both, I recommend the following steps:

1. Take a personal inventory of your eating habits. What foods or substances are you putting into your body that could be feeding into your battle with either depression or anxiety? Make a list of all the foods you are eating and liquids you are drinking and how much, including alcohol, tobacco, caffeinated drinks, processed foods with unnatural substances, enriched grains, fruits and vegetables, etc.

2. Put together a game plan on how to overcome addictions to certain substances, if you have them. Part of the plan should include consulting with a health professional to put together an eating strategy. If you have severe addictions to substances, such as drugs or alcohol or destructive habits like overeating, join a support group. It will be important to have people surrounding you who understand your situation and can provide support, because you will definitely need it. Poor eating habits can be an addiction as well. If you are eating poorly, eliminate the bad and put in the good substances. If you can't do this or are unsure of how to do this, seek help from a professional.

3. If you feel like snacking, replace candy or soda with something healthy like an apple, orange, or a drink of healthy juice (watch the sugar content though…a lot of the juices out there aren't as healthy as they appear). Have the new snacks in places where you kept the old ones. Make sure the old snacks are thrown away, so you don't have the temptation.

4. Tell friends and family members whom you trust and who you know will support you about your eating goals. See if they are willing to work on them with you. This will keep you accountable and also provide support for you.

5. Don't eat out—especially at fast-food places that have high amounts of processed, sugary foods. If you do eat out, make sure you know how they are preparing the foods and choose meals that are conducive to your eating goals. Ask the waiter

how many calories are in it, how the chef prepares the meal, etc.

6. Have a weekly meal plan. If you don't have a plan that fits your eating goals, it will be easier to fudge and go back to old habits.

7. Follow your meal plan. It's fine to have a plan, but it's only effective if you follow it. After you have written it, put it up somewhere you look at a lot, like the refrigerator, to remind you of your goals.

8. Put up pictures in your house that remind you of healthy eating and living. You could use pictures of people who look healthy and happy, pictures that remind you of good food, etc. The point is to get it into your subconscious so that you have a positive memory attached to eating healthy foods.

9. Eat small portions throughout the day as opposed to a few large meals. This stabilizes your blood sugar and helps keep your mind alert. It can also help stabilize your mood.

10. Before making any major changes, consult with a nutrition professional.

It is a wonder to me how many people struggle with depression and/or anxiety, yet continue to "self-medicate" by putting harmful substances into their bodies. This is a quick fix with a very negative long-term result. It isn't easy to kick poor eating habits and addictions, but it is a necessity for anyone who wants to overcome anxiety and depression. I've seen people, including myself, improve on their eating habits, and I know you can as well.

STEP 9: EXERCISE

Those who think they have not time for bodily exercise
will sooner or later have to find time for illness.
—Edward Stanley

One morning soon after I found out I was struggling with depression, I decided to pop in a yoga DVD. The program lasted about an hour and a half. As I followed the program, I found that my mind was focused on hitting the yoga poses correctly and my body was focused on balancing and breathing slowly, in and out. By the end of the workout, I felt completely peaceful and energized, which lasted a good portion of the day until my negative thoughts started coming (I hadn't yet had my mind trained to overcome the negative thoughts). I had always exercised, but after that day, I became a firm believer that exercise can help with overcoming anxiety and depression.

When I was training for triathlons, I was a college student and then a recent graduate only working part-time. I had time to train fifteen to twenty hours per week, and it felt great! However, after I "found a real job" and hit the workforce full-time, it was very hard for me to incorporate exercise into my daily routine. Furthermore, I started graduate school within a year of finishing my bachelor's degree, and it became even harder to exercise. I didn't like taking all the time to go to the gym and the fees involved, etc.

I was complaining about this to a friend one day when he introduced me to a program called Power 90 and P90X (see www.beachbody.com). This is an in-home training program that brings the gym to your home for not much more than it would cost for a gym membership. I knew that I needed to exercise not only to stay healthy physically but to help mentally with the anxiety and depression I was feeling. Therefore, I ordered the program.

Other than training for triathlons, the P90X program has helped me stay in the best shape I've ever been in. I was able to get a good workout in without having to take tons of time out of my busy sched-ule. I would wake up about a half hour earlier in the mornings and do the program. I gradually started feeling better about myself because of the energy I had from exercising. I started looking better as well, which also helped. Soon, people were commenting on how I was looking stronger and more fit, giving me positive feedback and good energy. I naturally felt like eating healthy food because the intensity of the workouts required good fuel for the body. Most important, I felt that it helped me curb the negative effects of anxiety and depres-sion.

LEARNING ACTIVITY

Some people are more motivated to exercise alone whereas oth-ers prefer to work out in groups or with another person. Whichever category you fall into, I encourage you to find some form of exercise that you enjoy. There are many kinds of exercise to consider. Look at the exercise strategies below, and then commit to applying at least one of them on a daily basis:

1. ***Join a gym***
   If your schedule allows, a gym is a wonderful place to go and has a variety of types of exercise areas available includ-ing swimming pools and basketball or racquetball courts, as well as various equipment like bicycles, weights, jogging machines, etc., and classes on aerobics and yoga. The other good thing about a gym is that you can associate with like-minded people in a spin or yoga class, in a racquetball game, etc. Although you may not be sitting there having conversa-tions, you are at least surrounding yourself with people who believe in improving their health and who are taking the steps to do so.

2. ***Join a local bike, running, or hiking club***
   Depending on the geography of where you live, there may be biking, running, and/or hiking clubs. When I was doing triathlons, I considered joining the local bike club. I prefer to exercise alone though, because it gives me time to clear my thoughts. When I talked with the club members, I found them

all to be very positive. They went on different trails a couple of times each week. If you are a social exerciser, then you should consider joining a club.

3. *In-Home Workout Program*
As mentioned, I use P90X (see www.beachbody.com) and have done so for a number of years. I've already described what I like about the program. Another program that I have recently looked at is the Supreme 90-Day workout (www.supreme90day.com). This is similar to Power 90, but it is a lot less expensive. Personally, I would go with the P90X, but if you are low on funds, the Supreme 90 is at least something to get you going.

The obvious downside to in-home programs is that you have to buy your weights, and if you don't have the space or desire to have weights in your home, this could be problematic. There are a lot of other in-home workouts though that do not require weights. Some I have used are yoga DVDs or exercise bands instead of weights.

4. *Get a Wii Fit*
I know people who love video games and who have a hard time making it to the gym. They may not prefer programs like P90X, so they use a Nintendo Wii Fit program to exercise.

5. *Get out and enjoy the sunshine*
If you live in an area where it is sunny, get out and clear your mind and thoughts as you take a walk. Do quick walks, jog, or run, whatever you are capable of doing, but just get out and get the endorphins and blood flowing at least twenty minutes to a half hour per day. You will notice a big difference, if you haven't already.

6. *Buy equipment for your home*
If you're like me, you prefer exercising alone, but you like a good workout. In the long run, it could save you money to purchase equipment if you have the room for it in your house. Personally, I would recommend buying a stationary bicycle,

elliptical, pull-up bar, yoga mat, exercise ball, and dumb-bells. With all of these, you can get a good cardio, weight, and stretching workout for your all-around health and not have to go to the gym.

7. ***Take up gardening***
Personally, I hate gardening. Maybe because of all the time I spent on the farm growing up I have it all out of my system. Those I see gardening seem to get a pretty good workout though. Mowing the lawn, digging, pulling, lifting—many of the activities you do with gardening are the same that a train-er would have you do at the gym.

8. ***Take the long way***
When I lived in Europe, everyone there made fun of Americans because we always drive everywhere we go and take eleva-tors. I didn't notice while I was growing up, but the Europeans were right. When I came back to the States after living in Eu-rope for a few years, I did notice how we sit in our cars wait-ing for the closest parking spot. We take the elevator and try to exert the least amount of energy possible. Making simple changes like taking the stairs or parking further away can give us much more exercise in the course of a day.

The following are a couple of tips to make your exercise more ef-fective, whichever strategy you choose.

Refer to the list on eating healthily in the previous chapter
It doesn't do much good if you exercise but keep eating junk foods. True, it is better to exercise even if you are eating junk than not to do anything at all, but the energy level you could be exerting is di-minished with an unhealthy diet. In order to gain complete health and positive energy, you must incorporate both a healthy diet and exercise.

Be consistent.
Exercising one day and then waiting a few days and doing it again is not very effective. It will not bring the results you want physically or emotionally. It is much better to do twenty to forty minutes daily and to do it four to six days a week.

This consistency is something that helps me each day to clear my mind and "get on track" emotionally. I also feel much better after the workout is finished because I have overcome my desire to stay in bed and worked toward a goal that I truly desire.

By following a regular exercise routine each day, I know that I can more easily manage and potentially overcome depression and anxiety. Exercising allows me to continue to feed my thoughts with positive energy, which is very crucial in reprogramming habitual negative thinking that leads to anxiety and depression.

STEP 10: GRATITUDE

Gratitude is deeper than thanks. Thankfulness is the beginning of gratitude. Gratitude is the completion of thankfulness. Thankfulness may consist merely of words. Gratitude is shown in acts.
—David O. McKay

I think it is human nature to be selfish, and for me at least, showing gratitude is something I have to make a conscious effort to do. It was especially difficult while I was struggling with anxiety and depression. For someone struggling with anxiety and depression, it can be difficult to sift through the clouds of doubt and discouragement that swirl like a tornado in the head. However, in order to steer the mind into a more positive direction, it is essential to see things in life for which you can be grateful.

The main thing that helped me learn gratitude during this time was keeping a journal of gratefulness. A good strategy to use is to write down things you are grateful for in a journal upon waking up in the morning and keep a notepad with you to jot down things that you are grateful for throughout the day. Right before going to bed, write in the journal again. This will keep the positive energy flowing throughout the day. Even if it's just simple things to be grateful for, every little bit of positive energy helps.

There are things to be grateful for all around us, if we take the time to look. You could focus on any of number of things. Just for the sake of example, I'll share some things I would write down.

In the morning, I would write, "I'm grateful I slept through the night without waking up. I'm grateful I feel healthy, have a job, have faith in God; I'm grateful for breakfast, for my family, for friends; I'm grateful I have enough money to buy nice clothes and good food, have a good home, etc..." The list goes on and on, but the point is to start the mind in a positive direction each morning. In addition to writing in the journal, I would pray and thank God for the things I wrote down.

Examples of things I would write down during the day may include, "I'm grateful that car let me in on the freeway and didn't cut me off, that my boss is nice to me, for my coworkers and the customers who appreciate good service, that I am valued at work, that I have a car to drive, for the good restaurants in our area that serve great lunch…" Again, the list goes on and on and is unique to each individual.

LEARNING ACTIVITY

Although this section is rather short, it is very important. The learning activity is also easy to describe, but it will take dedication to implement the strategy effectively.

First, buy a little notebook that you can carry around with you or a journal to keep handy with you throughout the day. Then, right when you get up in the morning, start writing down things you're grateful for. Even if it is only one thing, like you got a good night's rest or you were safe throughout the night while you slept, etc. Remember to jot down positive thoughts throughout the day in your journal or notepad.

Gratitude is crucial to overcoming stress and anxiety. As you do this activity, you will slowly notice that it becomes harder to have negative thoughts, and soon, you will see the world around you as a positive place.

STEP 11: RELAXATION

There is no need to go to India or anywhere else to find peace. You will find that deep place of silence right in your room, your garden, or even your bathtub.
—Elisabeth Kubler-Ross

Relaxing can be very hard for those who struggle with depression and especially anxiety. When the mind is trained to be constantly in overdrive, as minds of people with anxiety are, it is very hard to shut it off. In fact, trying to calm down can cause more stress on a person. I remember loaning my CDs to a friend who was struggling, only for him to give them back to me because it stressed him out too much to try to retrain his mind from following negative patterns.

Although it is hard to learn how to relax, it is very possible. On one occasion, I put in the relaxation CD from the Midwest Center for Stress and Anxiety program I had ordered as I was going to sleep at night. I noticed that I fell asleep rather quickly and slept soundly through the night for the first time in years. When I woke up the next morning, I noticed that I hadn't woken up, had bad dreams, or tossed and turned throughout the night. It was amazing!

Needless to say, learning relaxation strategies is a vital part of dealing with or recovering from anxiety and depression. When we are anxious, we're tense and our body follows where our minds take us. Relaxation of our minds leads to relaxation in our bodies and increases our overall well-being. Here are some tools to use when learning how to relax.

MUSIC
Music plays a powerful role in either making us more tense or relaxing us. Throughout my life, I have always loved hard rock music, but when I was struggling with depression and anxiety, I found that more melodic music like that of Enya, jazz, or classical music soothed

me during the day. At night, I would either listen to relaxation CDs or slow, mood-type music with ocean sounds, etc.

The trick is to focus on releasing tension in your muscles while you are listening to the music. Also, while you listen, do not let any negative thoughts enter your mind. Instead, just picture yourself in a relaxing place and focus on releasing tension in your muscles. What I found is that by putting on relaxing music and not only listening to it but focusing my thoughts around the melody and letting it carry me away, I eventually trained my mind to automatically relax every time I heard the music.

REIKI

I've already explained some of the benefits of Reiki along with providing the definition of what it is. When I would go to a Reiki therapist, I found that she could identify areas of tension that I was not aware of by focusing on my chakras. If one area was out of touch or too stressed, she would work to release the negative energy. The other thing I liked about attending the sessions is that the atmosphere was completely relaxing. There was a comfortable table to lie on, soft music playing, dim lights, and a little waterfall fountain. All of these things together would cause my body to totally relax, and I would usually fall into a very deep sleep. She would work on me as I slept for about an hour at a time, releasing all the negative tension and energy in my body. It was very therapeutic and crucial in learning how to relax.

YOGA

I discovered just how important relaxation strategies were soon after I found out I was suffering with depression and anxiety. On one occasion, I was doing yoga in my home with the new Power 90 videos I had just ordered. Before I started the session, I was nervous and struggling. However, I noticed that during my session and for a few hours after the session, my thoughts were clear and my tension and negative thoughts were gone.

Yoga is very good in the sense that you get a good workout, but you also have to concentrate and focus your thoughts and energy on balancing, or holding a pose, etc. I found that if I allowed my thoughts to wander, I would fall out of a pose and the workout would be ineffective.

Not only does it train you to focus your thoughts and energy, but it also provides a very good workout. I highly recommend adding at least one day of yoga into your exercise routine each week. If you are struggling a lot with depression or anxiety, I recommend doing yoga every other day, or about three days out of the week.

GUIDED IMAGERY

Guided imagery is a tool used to help relax and focus the mind through the help of someone guiding the patient with words. This can be done in person or through a recorded audio session.

Usually, I used the relaxation CD from the Midwest Stress Center, or a guided imagery session that was on another set of CDs I ordered from Jim Cox called "Becoming Spiritually Centered." Occasionally, I would have my Reiki therapist conduct a session, but usually, I would use the audio versions.

As I did when listening to music, I would put myself in a relaxing environment in my home, lie down in a comfortable location, focus my thoughts on what they were saying to me, and just let the images flow into my mind. Negative thoughts were uninvited, and when they came, I would picture myself opening up a door and letting them out.

At the height of my depression and anxiety, I would schedule about three or four times per day to have a guided imagery session for about fifteen minutes. If I was at work, I would just put in my headphones at my desk and close my eyes. If I was out and about, I would sit down somewhere, put in the session, and picture myself lying down on my bed or in another very relaxing place.

I found that over time guided imagery helped me also to focus my mind and train myself to be able to control the negative thoughts that led to anxiety and depression. It got to a point where I would put in the CD and my body would automatically relax and my mind would go to the relaxing place I had imagined before.

BREATHING

Breathing techniques are a crucial part of relaxation. When we have anxious thoughts, our heart rate and breathing increases and our bodies go into a "fight-or-flight" mode. However, if we consciously breathe slowly, we notice our heart rate decreases and it becomes easier to focus.

I found that breathing in deeply and slowly while counting five to seven seconds and then breathing out slowly counting five to seven seconds works very well, especially when combined with either a relaxation CD or some very relaxing music.

Controlled breathing is also very beneficial because you can do it anywhere and almost at any time. After practicing this technique for a few weeks, I noticed that when my anxious thoughts would come, if I didn't have any music handy, I could just stop what I was doing and start breathing in and out slowly, while playing the music I usually listened to in my mind.

MASSAGE

Anxiety wreaks havoc on your body. When I was struggling with anxiety and depression, it seemed as if all my muscles were tense and clenched 24/7. I would grit my teeth a lot, and so my face muscles were sore. My back carried a lot of tension as well.

Although I didn't get as many massages as I would have liked, when I did get a massage, all of that tension was released and it felt so freeing. If you have the means to get a massage on a regular basis, I highly recommend it. It is preferable to go to a professional massage therapy location. I recommend this for a couple of reasons. First, the relaxed environment with the soft, soothing music, dim lighting, and cool air help with relieving stress and clearing thoughts. Next, a massage therapist, especially one connected to or recommended by a doctor or chiropractor, understands how to do therapeutic massage. Finally, they have great equipment. The massage table alone is very comfortable, relaxing, and allows the body to be positioned in an ergonomically correct way while getting the massage.

Professional massages can be fairly expensive though, so if you have a significant other who can give you one regularly, I recommend being nice to that person—at least for as long as you want to get your massage! If you decide to go the "in-house" route with massages, make sure that you create a relaxing environment first. Buy massage lotion or oil, dim the lights, play relaxing music, and let your anxiety flow away.

A RELAXING ENVIRONMENT

I consider my environment to be both external and internal. In order to overcome anxiety and depression, it is crucial to learn how to create a relaxing internal environment. However, when first learning how to do this, it is often necessary to create a relaxing external environment first and allow the internal environment to follow. I'll share some examples.

When I was at the height of my anxiety and depression, I would get panic attacks fairly regularly. My internal environment was chaotic and not relaxed, to put it mildly. I would need to remove myself from the situation (external environment) I was in and put myself in a new, more relaxed situation. This can be easy to do if you're at home, but if you're at work or in a public place, it becomes much more difficult.

At home, if I was starting to feel anxiety, I learned to move immediately to a different location, such as my bed or a comfortable couch. I would then turn on some relaxing music or one of my relaxation CDs, close my eyes, and just focus on the music. Usually, after a few minutes, my mind would relax, and then my body would follow suit and relax as well.

Over time, my mind became conditioned to relax automatically when I heard the music or the relaxation CDs. This is beneficial because even if I was not at home but had access to the CDs (I recommend keeping one at your desk at work, in your car, on your iPod, etc.), I could still relax. Since my mind was used to telling my body to relax when it heard the music, my body would do so quickly and panic would leave. I was able to get to a point where all I had to do was think of the music in my mind, and my body would automatically respond regardless of my external environment.

The key to this strategy is making sure you consistently use the same music or relaxation CD. If you use various CDs, your body will not become conditioned to it. I recommend two to three variations and no more than that.

EXERCISE

Since I've dedicated a whole section to the various aspects of exercising, I won't go into much detail here. I will just say that exercising helps with removing anxiety, which can lead to depression, by helping us feel able to relax. I notice that if I don't exercise regularly, it is much harder for me to relax.

LIMITED MEDIA

Our minds are constantly being bombarded by marketing ads through our computers, TVs, radios, etc. In addition, we have instant access to multiple forms of media. If we are not careful, we can get consumed by all the shows, movies, ads, and other such stimuli. With all of this coming at us, it is important to reduce this chaos and clear our minds.

For me, I cut out watching TV altogether and had limited Internet use other than e-mails and doing personal things like banking and shopping online. I noticed that when I did this, it was much easier to keep my mind clear. However, reducing media was just the first step. The next step was to replace it with something enjoyable.

FINDING SOMETHING ENJOYABLE TO DO

I found that focusing too much on eliminating my anxiety or depression could be detrimental, since it caused me to focus on the problem excessively. Finding something enjoyable creates a place where you can escape and just let your mind be free. This can be any of numerous things, such as athletics, a good book, going out with friends, laughing (laughter is huge in reducing stress and anxiety), serving others, going back to school, joining a social club, and the list goes on.

My escape was usually something athletic, going out with friends, community service, studying, listening to or playing music, and reading self-improvement books.

Whatever it is you find enjoyable that isn't detrimental to your growth and health (like drugs, drinking, and the other things we've discussed that can lead to more stress and anxiety), do those activities in place of the normal activities you're accustomed to. I think you will be pleasantly surprised.

LEARNING ACTIVITY

Review each of the suggestions for learning to relax and incorporate any that you feel you would be interested in trying. The trick is not to overburden yourself with too many activities geared toward helping you relax. If you put too much on your plate, it will have a negative effect and cause even more stress. Just focus on however many truly bring you relaxation. For me, the three areas I would focus on would be: music, exercising, and breathing. You will need to experiment though because what worked for me may be a little different than what might work for you.

STEP 12: LAUGHTER

Laughter is the cure for grief.
—Robert Fulghum

Looking back on my journey of overcoming anxiety and depression, I see I could have benefited more from laughter. When I was going through severe anxiety and depression, it was very difficult to be happy because my mind was so weighed down by negativity and stress.

Although not taking life so seriously and laughing more often would have been good for me, I did have occasions where laughter helped me in a profound way. I noticed that when I laughed, the tension within my body relaxed as I felt the positive endorphins flowing. Even if I wasn't actually laughing but just enjoying myself, it made a huge difference.

There are several ways to find joy or laughter including spending time with good friends, playing games, laughing at your mistakes rather than beating yourself up over them, and watching a good sitcom or movie.

I'm sure there are many other ways to experience laughter and joy, but those are a few that helped me.

I encourage you to spend a few moments thinking of things that are more on the light and jovial side and then make an effort to put yourself in a position to experience them. It will make a huge difference in overcoming anxiety and depression.

EPILOGUE
LIFE AFTER ANXIETY AND DEPRESSION

Anxiety and depression didn't immediately vanish after I faced my demons. I continued to struggle for a little while after we were married and occasionally got a bit stressed out for larger events like our first pregnancy, and the birth of our first child.

Although the struggle with anxiety and depression didn't immediately vanish, it did eventually by continuing to utilize many of the twelve steps outlined in this book. I haven't had an anxiety attack in nearly five years and as I reflect on who I was and how I reacted during my struggles, it is almost as if I'm thinking about a completely different person.

By overcoming anxiety, I have achieved so many of my dreams such as having a family, having a flexible job that makes enough money to provide so my wife doesn't have to work, having means to provide support to various charities and friends and family members who struggle, participating as volunteers in our local congregation, being politically active, and athletically active in our communities. My life is something I could hardly even fathom when I was suffering from anxiety and depression. Instead of wanting to end my life, I feel like I want to embrace it and make the most out of every opportunity.

It is for this reason that I have written this book. Over the years I have had numerous people come up to me personally and ask for guidance in overcoming anxiety and depression. I've had many thousands more who have read my articles.

There is a life after overcoming anxiety and depression and it is my hope that something in this book guides you towards becoming the person you have always dreamt of being.

APPENDIX:
TEN HELPFUL BOOKS

THE TOP TEN BOOKS THAT HELPED ME LEARN TO CONTROL MY THOUGHTS

10. *Healing Depression & Bipolar Disorder without Drugs* by Grace- lyn Guyol

This book was loaned to me by my Reiki therapist. It is a very good, scientific reference on depression and includes various natural ways of healing depression, such as eating certain foods. I didn't make it through the whole book, as it was a bit too detailed and scientific for me, but it gave me a renewed hope that many people overcome depression without drugs.

9. *17 Lies that Are Holding You Back and the Truth that Will Set You Free* by Steve Chandler

The main quote I like from this book is: "Our thought habits de- termine the emotional lives we live" (p. 121). One thing I learned and grew to believe was that our circumstances don't just happen. They are created first within us and then are manifested through our ac- tions later. In my case, a panic attack followed by depression didn't just occur out of nowhere. It started with negative thought patterns. If I had positive thoughts, my feelings about myself and others were more positive.

8. *The Power of Your Subconscious Mind* by Joseph Murphy

This book opened my eyes to the fact that the manifestations of panic and depression I felt could be coming from my subconscious mind. This was a relief for me because I learned that it wasn't neces- sarily my fault that panic attacks and depression were happening to me. I learned that I was still a great person and not to hate myself or think of myself as weak for having the disorder. I also learned through this book that you can retrain your subconscious mind to think more positively about yourself and the world around you.

7. *The Law of Attraction* by Michael Losier

During my period of overcoming depression, many books that centered around the concept of the "law of attraction" became popular. The law of attraction, simply put, is that your thoughts create "vibrations," or feelings, which in turn attract more of the same. For example, if I had a negative thought and dwelled on that thought, it escalated and more and more negative "vibrations" were created until I had a panic attack. However, if I thought positive, uplifting thoughts, the opposite would happen, and I would become happy and joyful rather than afraid and depressed.

What I liked about this book is that it contained learning activities and worksheets to help me overcome negative thought patterns as well. It trained me to turn negative thought habits into positive ones.

6. *The Magic of Thinking Big* by David Schwartz

The chapters in this book almost speak for themselves: "Believe You Can Succeed and You Will"; "Build Confidence and Destroy Fear"; "You Are Who You Think you Are"; "How to Turn Defeat into Victory"; etc.

5. *The Jackrabbit Factor* by Leslie Householder

I went to a seminar given by Leslie Householder (www.thought-salive.com) and was very impressed. She shared her personal story of struggle and learning how to overcome her negative thought patterns. She presented many concepts and examples similar to those in the *Law of Attraction* in her seminar and in her book. She also referenced a book that became one of the main books I read, reread, and read again called *As a Man Thinketh*.

4. *Think and Grow Rich* by Napoleon Hill

This book is an excellent source of guidance for individuals looking to improve any facet of their lives. As the title suggests, riches (which can be money, happiness—basically whatever we deem to be valuable) come as a result of the thoughts we have. Below are some great quotes from the author:

"Our brains become magnetized with the dominating thoughts which we hold in our minds, and, by means with which no man is familiar, these "magnets" attract to us the forces, the people, the circumstances of life which harmonize with the nature of our dominating thoughts."

"Effort only fully releases its reward after a person refuses to quit."

"Most great people have attained their greatest success just one step beyond their greatest failure."

"Self-discipline begins with the mastery of your thoughts. If you don't control what you think, you can't control what you do. Simply, self-discipline enables you to think first and act afterward."

The list goes on and on, but as you can see, Napoleon Hill was ahead of his time and a very inspiring and motivating individual. This book helped and continues to help me focus my thoughts on positive things and remove the negative things.

3. *The Science of Getting Rich* by Wallace D. Wattles

When I thought of "richness," I envisioned a life in which I had a flexible job that allowed me to spend time with my family and travel. I pictured a clear mind and confident spirit. I saw a loving wife and beautiful children. I also pictured making enough money not only to support my own family but to help support those around me. This book helped me create a vision and understand more deeply the law of attraction, which states the thoughts we think manifest themselves in our lives. I learned from this book that, when setting goals, you need to focus on abundance and what you want, rather than focusing on what you lack. This book, like *Think and Grow Rich* has many, many great quotes. I'll share a few with you:

"The object of all life is development; and everything that lives has an inalienable right to all the development it is capable of attaining."

"There are three motives for which we live; we live for the body, we live for the mind, we live for the soul. No one of these is better or holier than the other; all are alike desirable, and no one of the three—body, mind, or soul—can live fully if either of the others is cut short of full life and expression."

"...you can render to God and humanity no greater service than to make the most of yourself."

"Like causes must produce like effects."

"Since belief is all important, it behooves you to guard your thoughts; and as your beliefs will be shaped to a very great extent by the things you observe and think about, it is important that you should command your attention."

"The moment you permit your mind to dwell with dissatisfaction upon things as they are, you begin to lose ground."

"The Creative Power within us makes us into the image of that to which we give our attention. We are Thinking Substance, and thinking substance always takes the form of that which it thinks about."

"Thinking in a Certain Way will bring riches to you, but you must not rely upon thought alone, paying no attention to personal action...man must not only think, but his personal action must supplement his thought."

I could go on and on with quotes from this book, but needless to say, the suggestions were very helpful, and I made the effort to apply them in my life. As I did so, my thoughts become more positive and I gained a clear vision of what I wanted out of life. It took time. In fact, it took many years. However, as I held on to the vision of living a life with clear thoughts and positive relationships, slowly but surely, it began to manifest itself.

2. Scriptures (Book of Mormon, Bible, Doctrine and Covenants)

I believe that God speaks to us in many ways. He speaks to us through other people, feelings in our hearts, impressions in our minds, and also through scripture. I've learned that as I read and study scripture, I learn more about myself as well as God. Three books of scripture helped me when I was at my lowest points of depression by teaching me more about myself as well as providing a vision of how to improve my life. The books were: the Book of Mormon, the Bible, and the Doctrine and Covenants.

1) Book of Mormon: We have same Spirit after we die.

Alma Chapter 34: 32–34 in the Book of Mormon was what kept me moving ahead. It states that the purpose for this life is to prepare us to meet God and that there comes a time when we cannot prepare to meet God anymore. It also states that the same spirit we have within our bodies will be the one we have after we die.

When I was at my lowest point, thoughts of suicide would come to me. I would sometimes entertain the idea of how much easier my burden would be if I could just not be living. However, as I contemplated that, I would reflect on this scripture, and I came to realize that death would not be an escape but a continuation of my current troubles and most likely even worse. Ending my life was not something I wanted to be held accountable for when I stood before God either. Therefore, I chose to keep looking forward.

2) The Bible: "As a Man Thinketh in his Heart so is He" (Proverbs 23:7)

The Bible tells us in a few places that one's actions are a reflection of one's heart (which I understand to be one's inner thoughts and desires). The first is in Proverbs 23 and simply states: "As a man thinketh in his heart, so is he." The next is in Matthew 15 where Jesus discusses how the things that come forth from the heart can defile a man and lead to other things, such as fornication, adultery, murder, and evil thoughts.

These scriptures were very inspirational for me as I examined my outward behavior and thought patterns and worked toward overcoming my struggles with anxiety and depression. As I reflected, I realized that my negative thoughts led to more negative thoughts, which then led to negative outward actions in many cases and manifested themselves through panic attacks and depressive episodes. I had consistently trained my mind to think negatively and had to work very, very hard at being more conscious of my thoughts. I accomplished this by writing down negative thoughts as they occurred and then writing down a positive one to replace each negative one. I also grew to realize as well that in my situation, the negative thoughts were coming from my subconscious mind. I learned I needed to address reprogramming my subconscious mind and was able to accomplish that, which will be discussed later.

3) Doctrine and Covenants: "Light cleaves to light."

In the Doctrine and Covenants 130:20–21, it says:

There is a law, irrevocably decreed in heaven before the foundations of this world, upon which all blessings are predicated—And when we obtain any blessing from God, it is by obedience to that law upon which it is predicated.

This scripture means that there are laws that when followed ensure that God will bless you. Some examples could include the law of loving other people. If we learn to love others, we are blessed with a greater peace in our hearts. There is also the law of giving. When we give from our hearts, others are blessed, but God inevitably blesses the giver as well. I had heard this scripture before and seen the positive effects of obedience to certain laws. However, when I heard it quoted by Bob Proctor in the documentary about the book *The Secret*, I discovered another law I had not been following.

Proctor discusses the law of attraction, which essentially states that like things will be attracted to each other. For example, the positive or negative things we think about will be attracted to us and ultimately manifested in our lives.

This concept was not new to me because I had often read in the past in scripture that there are laws with certain bounds and conditions where "light cleaves to light, intelligence cleaves to intelligence, truth embraces truth, virtue loves virtue..." (Doctrine and Covenants 88:38–40).

As I reflected on these scriptures, I decided that I wanted to become a better me. I wanted to love myself and feel comfortable in my own skin. I wanted a healthy relationship with a good woman and a family. I wanted to be successful in a career and have money for my family and also to help those in need. I wanted to be the best "me" that I could be. I knew that it would start with reprogramming the way I thought about myself and the world around me. I believed that once I learned how to think more positively, through the law of attraction, God would bring positive things into my life.

1. *As a Man Thinketh* by James Allen

I read and reread this book consistently over the course of the couple of years that it took for me to rid myself of my thoughts of anxiety, which led to depression. I agree with Leslie Householder when she challenges the reader to read this book, underline the significant and impactful statements, and see if there is any part of the book that isn't underlined. However, I have included seventeen quotes from the book that I feel were instrumental in helping me retrain my thought patterns from negative to positive.

Seventeen Helpful Quotes from* As a Man Thinketh *that Reshaped My Thinking

1. "A man is *literally* what he thinks. His character is the complete sum of *all his thoughts.*"
2. "Only by much searching and mining are gold and diamonds obtained, and man can find every truth connected with his being if he will dig deep into the mine of his soul."
3. "A man's mind may be likened to a garden, which may be intelligently cultivated or allowed to run wild; but whether cultivated or neglected, it *must and will bring forth*. If no useful seeds are put into it, then an abundance of useless weed seeds will *fall* therein and will continue to produce their kind."
4. "The soul attracts that which it secretly harbors; that which it loves and also that which it fears."
5. "Circumstance does not make the man, it reveals him to himself."
6. "Men are anxious to improve their circumstances, but are unwilling to improve themselves. They therefore remain bound."
7. "Man is the cause (though nearly always unconsciously) of his circumstances."
8. "Good thoughts and actions can never produce bad results. Bad thoughts and actions can never produce good results.

This is but saying that nothing can come from corn but corn, nothing from nettles but nettles."

9. "Men imagine that thought can be kept secret, but it cannot. It rapidly crystallizes into habit, and habit solidifies into habits of drunkenness and sensuality, which solidify into circumstances of destitution and disease. Impure thoughts of every kind crystallize into enervating and confusing habits, which solidify into distracting and adverse circumstances. Thoughts of fear, doubt, and indecision crystallize into weak, unmanly, and irresolute habits, which solidify into circumstances of failure, indigence, and slavish dependence."

10. "A man cannot *directly* choose his circumstances, but he can choose his thoughts and so indirectly, yet surely, shape his circumstances."

11. "If you would perfect your body, guard your mind. Out of a clean heart comes a clean life and clean body."

12. "Until thought is linked with purpose there is no intelligent accomplishment."

13. "A man should conceive of a legitimate purpose in his heart, and set out to accomplish it. He should make this purpose the centralizing point of his thoughts. It may take the form of a spiritual ideal, or it may be a worldly object, according to his nature at the time being. But whichever it is, he should steadily focus his thought forces upon the object which he has set before him. He should make this purpose his supreme duty, and should devote himself to its attainment, not allowing his thoughts to wander away into ephemeral fancies, longings, and imaginings."

14. "As the physically weak man can make himself strong by careful and patient training, so the man of weak thoughts can make them strong by exercising himself in right thinking."

15. "Thought allied fearlessly to purpose becomes creative force."

16. "A man's condition is his own and not another man's. His suffering and his happiness are evolved from within. As he thinks, so he is, as he continues to think, so he remains."

17. "He who has conquered weakness, and has put away all selfish thoughts...is free."

These quotes helped me realize that my thoughts had shaped who I had become, and it was very freeing to realize this. I understood that subconsciously, I sabotaged relationships with women. I learned that I had been engaging in negative self-talk that manifested itself through anxiety and depression. I also realized that I could turn it around through patiently surrounding myself with positive things externally, such as true friends, good pictures in my home, etc., and most important by being conscious of what I internalized through the music I listened to and the books I read. I learned that it was okay that I had felt this way and it was natural because I had simply let my thoughts run wild. It was time to "weed" out my habitual negative thoughts and create a vision and reason for changing.

For me, the vision and purpose I had was that I simply wanted to be free of anxiety and depression. I wanted to feel what life was like without the burden and weight that anxiety and depression laid on me. I saw other "normal" people and longed to be happy like they were. I believed with all my heart that I could do it. It took a lot of work, but today, when people see me, they have no clue that I suffered from anxiety and depression. I'm sure they look at me and, in the words of James Allen, have no "knowledge of the sacrifice I made… the undaunted efforts I needed to put forth and the faith I exercised so I could overcome the insurmountable, and realize the Vision of my heart."

LEARNING ACTIVITY

Carefully read *As a Man Thinketh* by James Allen. A free copy of the book can be found on Leslie Householder's website: thoughtsalive.com. Underline portions of the book that stand out to you. After you have read the book, look at what you have underlined and then make an action plan on how you will apply your goals in your life. Order a copy of the suggested books as well. Each author has a different take on things that will help you.

For part of your action plan, write it up on a board or somewhere else where you can review it daily. As you are reviewing your goals daily, remember to take time to visualize how life will be once you have obtained the goal. How will you feel? How will others around you feel? What will life look like?

Once you have read *As a Man Thinketh* and created a vision board, read other books or articles that pertain to your vision. Hold on to this vision, and it will begin to manifest itself in your life over time.

ABOUT THE AUTHOR

Aaron Anderson is a husband and father of two children. He holds Masters Degrees in Business and Organizational Leadership and is a sales and marketing professional. He actively supports organizations such as the American Diabetes Association, American Red Cross, Perpetual Education Fund, and LDS Philanthropies.

Through overwhelming responses to articles he has written on overcoming anxiety and depression, he was encouraged to write this book. His writings have been able to help thousands of people with overcoming anxiety and depression.

Made in the USA
San Bernardino, CA
16 March 2015